Emily Huntington

**The Cooking Garden**

A systematized course of cooking for pupils of all ages, including plan of work, bills of fare, songs, and letters of information

Emily Huntington

**The Cooking Garden**
*A systematized course of cooking for pupils of all ages, including plan of work, bills of fare, songs, and letters of information*

ISBN/EAN: 9783744785341

Printed in Europe, USA, Canada, Australia, Japan

Cover: Foto ©Lupo / pixelio.de

More available books at **www.hansebooks.com**

# THE COOKING GARDEN.

## A SYSTEMATIZED COURSE OF COOKING

### FOR PUPILS OF ALL AGES,

INCLUDING

PLAN OF WORK, BILLS OF FARE, SONGS, AND
LETTERS OF INFORMATION.

ARRANGED BY

EMILY HUNTINGTON.

WHAT IS THE USE OF A DAUGHTER AT HOME,
IF FOR A GOOD DINNER A FATHER MUST ROAM?

ILLUSTRATED BY JESSIE SHEPHERD.

V

*Only 250 Copies for Subscribers.*

No. 37

COPYRIGHT, 1885,
BY EMILY HUNTINGTON.

Press of J. J. Little & Co.,
Nos. 10 to 20 Astor Place, New York.

New York: J. W. Schermerhorn & Co.,
7 East 14th Street.
1885.

BY PERMISSION,

I RESPECTFULLY AND GRATEFULLY

DEDICATE

TO THE

BOARD OF MANAGERS

OF THE

WILSON INDUSTRIAL SCHOOL

(THE PIONEER IN INDUSTRIAL WORK FOR GIRLS),

THIS SEQUEL

TO MY

KITCHEN GARDEN,

BOTH OF THESE SYSTEMS HAVING BEEN
DEVELOPED IN THEIR SERVICE.

# Introduction.

"IT WAS NOT LIKE A SCHOOL-ROOM AT ALL."

How does the Cooking Garden differ from other systems?

It begins at the first cooking principles where the Kitchen Garden leaves off.

It is adapted to children as well as adults. It believes in many small centres rather than in large note-taking audiences. Its pupils work out with their own hands each lesson under intelligent guidance.

The cost of materials for each lesson is very small. It uses all parts of the stove during each lesson. It centres attention on one principal article of food till thoroughly understood at each lesson. It works from receipt charts or blackboards in sight of all the class.

It saves the time of the pupils by teacher's previous convenient arrangement of utensils and material. It finishes its instructions by training pupils to arrange bills of fare with the proper combinations.

Also to calculate time to cook and bring the dishes to a serving-point at the right moment during the meal.

# Contents.

|  | PAGE |
|---|---|
| Dedication | 3 |
| Introduction | 5 |
| Letter to Teachers | 11 |
| Utensils necessary for a Class | 13 |
| Introductory Letter to Pupils | 15 |

**LESSON FIRST—**

| Bill of Fare | 19 |
|---|---|
| Utensils Required | 19 |
| Material Required | 19 |
| Expense of Material | 19 |
| Order of Exercises | 21 |
| Letter of Information | 23 |
| Questions on the Lesson | 25 |
| Receipts | 26 |
| Milk Toast | 26 |
| Welsh Rarebit | 26 |
| Queen Toast | 26 |
| Water Toast | 26 |
| Toast Crumbs | 27 |
| Recapitulation of the Lesson | 27 |
| Diagram for arrangement of Cooking-tables | 29 |

**LESSON SECOND—**

| Bill of Fare | 33 |
|---|---|
| Utensils Required | 33 |
| Material Required | 33 |
| Expense of Material | 33 |
| Order of Exercises | 35 |
| Letter of Information | 37 |
| Questions on the Lesson | 39 |
| Receipts | 41 |
| Mashed Potatoes | 41 |
| Stewed Potatoes | 41 |
| Fried Potatoes | 41 |
| Stuffed Potatoes | 41 |
| Riced Potatoes | 41 |
| Recapitulation of the Lesson | 42 |
| Diagram for arrangement of Cooking-tables | 44 |

## CONTENTS

**LESSON THIRD—**   PAGE
- Bill of Fare .................................................. 47
- Utensils Required .......................................... 47
- Material Required .......................................... 47
- Expense of Material ........................................ 47
- Order of Exercises ......................................... 49
- Letter of Information ...................................... 51
- Questions on the Lesson .................................... 52
- Receipts ................................................... 54
- Scrambled Eggs ............................................. 54
- Baked Omelet ............................................... 54
- Poached Eggs ............................................... 54
- Quaker Omelet .............................................. 54
- Plain Omelet ............................................... 54
- Recapitulation of the Lesson ............................... 55
- Diagram for arrangement of Cooking-tables .................. 57

**LESSON FOURTH—**
- Bill of Fare ............................................... 61
- Utensils Required .......................................... 61
- Material Required .......................................... 61
- Expense of Material ........................................ 61
- Order of Exercises ......................................... 63
- Letter of Information ...................................... 65
- Questions on the Lesson .................................... 67
- Receipts ................................................... 70
- Roast Beef ................................................. 70
- Fried Steak ................................................ 70
- Mock Duck .................................................. 70
- Broiled Steak .............................................. 70
- Breaded Chops .............................................. 71
- Recapitulation of the Lesson ............................... 71
- Diagram for arrangement of Cooking-tables .................. 74

**LESSON FIFTH—**
- Bill of Fare ............................................... 77
- Utensils Required .......................................... 77
- Material Required .......................................... 77
- Expense of Material ........................................ 77
- Order of Exercises ......................................... 79
- Letter of Information ...................................... 81
- Questions on the Lesson .................................... 82
- Receipts ................................................... 83
- Corned Beef Hash ........................................... 83

## CONTENTS.

|   | PAGE |
|---|---|
| Hash on Toast | 83 |
| Warmed-over Meat | 83 |
| Meat Escaloped | 83 |
| Recapitulation of the Lesson | 83 |
| Diagram for arrangement of Cooking-tables | 86 |

**LESSON SIXTH—**
- Bill of Fare ... 89
- Utensils Required ... 89
- Material Required ... 89
- Expense of Material ... 90
- Order of Exercises ... 91
- Letter of Information ... 93
- Questions on the Lesson ... 95
- Receipts ... 97
- Bread ... 97
- French Rolls ... 97
- Powder Biscuit ... 97
- Fried Dough ... 97
- Cinnamon Bread ... 98
- Recapitulation of the Lesson ... 98
- Diagram for arrangement of Cooking-tables ... 100

**LESSON SEVENTH—**
- Bill of Fare ... 103
- Utensils Required ... 103
- Material Required ... 103
- Expense of Material ... 103
- Order of Exercises ... 105
- Letter of Information ... 107
- Questions on the Lesson ... 108
- Receipts ... 109
- Minced Spinach ... 109
- Cream Carrots ... 109
- Fried Parsnips ... 109
- Escaloped Tomatoes ... 109
- Recapitulation of the Lesson ... 109
- Diagram for arrangement of Cooking-tables ... 112

**LESSON EIGHTH—**
- Bill of Fare ... 115
- Material Required ... 115
- Expense of Material ... 115
- Utensils Required ... 116
- Order of Exercises ... 117

## CONTENTS.

|  | PAGE |
|---|---|
| Letter of Information | 119 |
| Questions on the Lesson | 120 |
| Receipts | 122 |
| Broiled Fish | 122 |
| Boiled Fish | 122 |
| Fried Fish | 122 |
| Baked Fish | 122 |
| Flaked Fish | 122 |
| Recapitulation of the Lesson | 123 |
| Diagram for arrangement of Cooking-tables | 125 |

### LESSON NINTH—

|  |  |
|---|---|
| Bill of Fare | 129 |
| Utensils Required | 129 |
| Material Required | 129 |
| Expense of Material | 129 |
| Order of Exercises | 131 |
| Letter of Information | 133 |
| Questions on the Lesson | 134 |
| Receipts | 136 |
| Tomato Soup | 136 |
| Bean Soup | 136 |
| Potato Soup | 136 |
| Pea Soup | 136 |
| Stock | 136 |
| Recapitulation of the Lesson | 137 |
| Diagram for arrangement of Cooking-tables | 139 |

### LESSON TENTH—

|  |  |
|---|---|
| Bill of Fare | 143 |
| Material Required | 143 |
| Expense of Material | 143 |
| Utensils Required | 144 |
| Order of Exercises | 145 |
| Letter of Information | 147 |
| Questions on the Lesson | 147 |
| Receipts | 149 |
| Bread Pudding | 149 |
| Rice Pudding | 149 |
| Baked Custard | 149 |
| Boiled Custard | 149 |
| Lemon Pudding | 149 |
| Corn-starch Blanc-mange | 150 |
| Recapitulation of the Lesson | 150 |
| Diagram for arrangement of Cooking-tables | 153 |

# To the Teacher.

DEAR FRIEND:—

This book is for those who are anxious to teach simple cooking, in classes. The world is full of cook-books, with excellent receipts, easily adapted to this system. What I have tried to do, is to help you to a plan of work. The letters to scholars you can put into your own words, and give as your own, or you can say, " Miss Huntington's letter given in connection with this lesson is as follows." It was a pleasant thought that I might be able to teach many pupils, even at a distance. The lessons are planned for a class of twelve (12) to be really at work, and any number looking on. Lessons can be given in any room, and a wardrobe can be used to hold the utensils, the doors of which can be arranged to unhinge and lay on trestles, and used as work-tables ; while the stove can be set on castors, for convenience in moving it. But a kitchen garden room is best, and to have the children march in and sit at kitchen garden tables. Then, if the same lesson is given four (4) times, and the receipts changed to different girls, all the twelve (12) at work will have tried each of the four receipts, and all the class have the benefit of the others' practice.

I have uniform aprons for the scholars, and also for the young lady teachers. A reliable char-woman comes in at the close of each lesson to put things to rights. In evening classes, when girls are taught who are at work during the day, I have not thought it best to keep them a moment after the lesson to wash up the dishes and put each in its place.

If the lessons are too long they tire both teacher and pupils, and spoil the effect. So, I have a diagram of the room, and topics to work by, that all may be arranged when the lesson begins ; and the receipt charts should be on the wall, and the materials ready to start the lesson the moment the pupils march into the room. An hour and a half should be the outside limit of a lesson.

In the Order of Exercises you will see "Songs" are referred to. I have found songs with hints and rules in them *very* useful, in teaching children especially. As turning over leaves is inconvenient, I have had the cooking songs printed on large cards. The teacher's apparatus consists of the Teacher's Manual, the long cards, and the receipt charts. At the close of the lesson I have had the cooked dishes arranged on a tray and placed in front of the teacher for suggestions and comments from her, while the class marched in review past the table, after which the pupils were allowed to eat or carry home samples of the food; this adds greatly to the enthusiasm of the lesson.

Then the dishes to be washed were carried to the sink, all the scholars marching together, as seen in the illustration at the close of this book, and the class dismissed. Each course of lessons must vary and be adapted to place and circumstances.

To some teachers, the rhyming songs may seem useless, if not foolish; but I have found them valuable, even with girls twenty (20) years of age, in keeping the class in order, and their minds on the lesson, while waiting for a kettle to boil or a cake to bake. Appoint a special one to take charge of the fire or dish in the meantime, that nothing be spoiled.

I trust these lessons may encourage others to undertake to teach what is so important and so practical. And also that they may furnish innocent amusement for young persons during hours otherwise idle, when the great Tempter of souls is alert.

Yours in full sympathy,<br>E. HUNTINGTON.

# Utensils Necessary For Class of Twelve Pupils.

### IRON WARE.

Stove,
Kettle,
Dripping-pan and Rack,
Porcelain-lined Kettle and Cover,
Gridiron,
Three Frying-pans and Covers,
Two Saucepans and Covers,
Two Square Loaf-pans,
One Pan for Biscuits,
One Pan for Rolls,
Two Spiders,
Two Pots,
One Toaster.

### TIN WARE.

Saucepan and Cover,
Large Pitcher,
Dredging-boxes,
Quart Measure, with Divisions,
Nutmeg-grater,
Twelve Small Pans,
Large Grater,
Colander,
Skimmer,
Strainer,
Sieve,
Two Pails.

## WOODEN WARE.

Board to stand hot kettles upon,
Two Moulding-boards,
Twelve Small Table-boards,
Two Chopping-bowls,
Two Rolling-pins,
Two Water-pails,
Wooden Spoons.

## CROCKERY.

Four Dishes — meat — different sizes,
Four Vegetable-dishes,
Two Quart Bowls,
One Small Bowl,
One Quart Pitcher,
One Pint Pitcher,
Six Cups,
Six Plates,
One Baking-dish.

## CUTLERY.

Twelve Paring-knives,
Six Kitchen Knives,
Twelve Kitchen Forks,
Four Toasting-forks,
One Dozen Table-spoons.

## LINEN.

Half Dozen Towels,
Half Dozen Holders.
One Cloth to boil Fish in.

The outfit, with the exception of the stove, can be purchased by the above list. If the demand is sufficient, tin trunks containing a complete set will be for sale at the Kitchen Garden Agency.

My Dear Young Friends:—

It is very pleasant to me to be able to give you cooking lessons. You will enjoy them very much. It makes such a difference in a home if you know how things should be done, and the surest way to keep people good natured in a family is to give them good things to eat.

It is quite right that it should be so, and it is especially due to those who earn the money to buy the food that they should enjoy it when put on to the table ; and it is no harder to learn to cook well than it is to cook ill.

I am not attempting elaborate or fine cooking, so you will not expect it, at least not at present, but I will show you some nice ways of preparing ordinary dishes.

Now, in the first place you need to know how to manage a fire, for if you fail in that you will fail in your cooking ; therefore, you must understand all about the dampers, and in buying a stove one should learn at the shop how and when to open and close them.

When you start your fire the dampers should all be open.

Do not lay paper flat in the fire basket, but twist it in bunches, putting in first the paper, then kindlings so crossed as to let the air draw through, placing the heavier pieces of wood upon the top.

As soon as *all* are well burning add two or three shovelfuls of coal. It is better to feed the fire often at first, but by the time you are ready to cook it must be a solid fire, that will last through the lesson.

Now as to cooking utensils. As far as we can we will use those made of iron, because they are stronger and cheaper than any other kind, and if perfectly clean will grow better all the time. They should always be dried thoroughly after washing, and put away without their lids, and with their faces down. Something should raise them sufficiently to let in the air, as the cleanest saucepan will smell musty if left in such a way that the air cannot reach the inside of it.

An iron dripping pan, such as meat is roasted in, should be carefully cleaned with an iron dish cloth and soda, instead of soap, as the least trace of former cooking will give a fresh piece of meat a bad flavor.

The last thing you should do before begining to cook is to wash your hands and clean your nails.

I have known many girls who have had to take their mother's place when very young, and learn to cook for their fathers and little brothers and sisters.

If a child's bones are not quite hard before it is seven years of age it will never be strong, and its legs will be crooked and weak; and every woman should understand the nature of food for the sake of those under her care.

The quality of food intended for little children should be carefully studied, as the firmness of their flesh and the hardness of their bones is so dependent upon it.

A man is able to work longer and better if his meals are nourishing. He does not know when to add salt or pepper, and why should he? It should be the care of the wife or daughter to so season the food that the first mouthful is appetizing.

The body requires animal, vegetable, and mineral food. Vegetables draw the mineral matter from the soil and change it into food, part of which is used directly by man and part eaten by animals, and thus is converted into more strengthening food for him.

Milk contains all the essential elements for the support of human life, and flour is one of the most nourishing forms of vegetable food. It has in it albumen or gluten which makes the muscles and the nerves; starch and sugar which make fat; gelatine and the minerals, lime and phosphorus, which make the bones grow strong and hard. Children who have cut all their teeth will thrive well and grow strong if they eat heartily of good bread every day. Home-made bread should be eaten in preference to baker's bread, because in baker's bread some of those valuable nutritive parts are destroyed, and while it satisfies hunger it does not nourish the body.

Salt is necessary, and yet those who live entirely upon salted meat are apt to have a disease which the use of fresh vegetables will cure.

Fruit helps to purify the blood. Fish feeds the brain, and the cereals, such as wheat, corn, and rye, also.

Do not expect success at first, and it would be a mistake to attempt receipts so expensive that you could not repeatedly try them, and by patient effort bring satisfactory results at last. All the receipts of this course will be simple and inexpensive.

Yours sincerely,<br>
E. Huntington.

# LESSON FIRST.

THE LITTLE COOKS AT WORK.

# FIRST COOKING LESSON.

## BILL OF FARE.

MILK TOAST.

WELSH RARE-BIT.

QUEEN TOAST.

WATER TOAST.

TOAST CRUMBS.

*Utensils Required.*

| | |
|---|---|
| 12 Table Boards. | 6 Plates for Bread. |
| 12 Knives. | 1 Pint Measure. |
| 3 Forks. | 1 Egg Beater. |
| 2 Teaspoons. | 1 Grater. |
| 2 Teacups. | 1 Skimmer. |
| 1 Bowl. | 1 Toasting Fork. |
| 2 Deep Dishes. | 1 Spider. |
| 1 Small Platter. | 1 Baking Pan. |
| 2 Covered Dishes. | 1 Saucepan. |

MATERIAL REQUIRED.

| | |
|---|---|
| 3 Pints of Milk.................................. | $0 12 |
| 2 Eggs ............................................ | 07 |
| 1½ Loaves of Bread ........................ | 12 |
| ½ Lb. of Butter. .............................. | 18 |
| ½ Lb. of Lard................................... | 07 |
| Flour, Pepper, and Salt................ | 01 |
| Sugar and Cinnamon .................. | 02 |
| ¼ Lb. of Cheese............................. | 06 |
| | $0 65 |

# Order of Exercises.

MARCH.

CHORD—BE SEATED.

Song—"*We want to be Cheerful.*"

*Lecture.*

*A few Questions.*

Song—"*Home Welcome.*"

*Read Bill of Fare.*

Appoint three girls to each receipt.
Start girls cutting bread, and explain how.   Teacher show the way.
When bread is cut, let as many toast as there is room for at the stove.
Have cheese grated and egg beaten.
Put milk on to heat, and prepare thickening.
Place frying-pan on the stove, heat butter and lard, and fry bread.
Put toast crumbs in the oven.
When the meal is prepared, class be seated and taste.
Review of questions.

# A LETTER ON THE USES OF STALE BREAD.

This lesson is to give you a few ideas on the uses of *stale bread*.

People who buy bread every day are not apt to have it stale, but when it is made at home once or twice a week, there are often pieces left over, and it is desirable to know good ways of making use of them.

We all wish to be economical house-keepers. Some people think that to be economical is to be mean, but this is a great mistake.

It means only to make the best use of what we have, for " wilful waste makes woful want."

To be wasteful through ignorance is no less wrong, especially if we have a chance to learn how to do better.

Some baker's bread can be bought at about half price, and when made into a nice dish of Milk Toast, or Welsh Rare-bit, it is a very inviting dish for supper.

*Milk Toast* to be nice must be crisp, brown, and tender, but not so soft that the cream will soak into it; and care should be taken that the milk be in readiness when the toast is made, so that the toast will not have time to steam before the milk is poured over it.

The only difference between *Milk Toast* and *Welsh Rare-bit* is in the dressing, which for the latter contains a little grated cheese and an egg.

Gentlemen usually enjoy this dish, so if you are ever allowed to prepare a dish for your father, and he enjoys *cheese*, suppose you try this one.

*Cream Dressing* should not be quite so thick as condensed milk, but a little thicker than common cream.

Corn-starch or flour may be used as thickening, and sometimes we use an egg for the same purpose.

Eggs are also used to make food light and keep it from absorbing fat.

When used to thicken, the whites and gold need not be separated. They should be chopped rather than beaten.

When used to make your cooking light and puffy, the whites and yelks should be beaten separately.

We beat them with long beats, so that the little cells may be filled with air.

When sugar, or anything, is added, beat it in sideways with a spoon, so that these air-cells may not be broken.

To make *Water Toast* the bread should be nicely browned, then dipped quickly in salted water. Do not spread butter over it, but place little bits to melt; this prevents the toast being broken.

*Queen Toast* is made by soaking the slices in a very plain uncooked custard, and browning in a frying-pan. When served, sugar and cinnamon are sprinkled between the slices as they are piled upon the dish.

If you have a large family to toast for, you can get on faster if you lay the slices on the rack in the oven to dry a little, while the first pieces are being prepared.

Toast can be made *over* a clean grate fire, but it is nicer when held *before* the fire.

In making toast for a sick person, never hold it *over* the fire, as it is not nearly as delicate.

*Toast Crumbs* are made of buttered bread cut in very small cubes, and placed in the oven to brown. These are very nice served with soup, and it is a good way to use up very small pieces of bread.

*Stale Bread* may be laid aside until thoroughly dried, then rolled very fine. Put this into a wide-mouthed bottle into which you can dip a spoon. This is useful in many ways, as in breading veal chops or oysters.

In serving dry toast, the slices should not be piled one upon another, but placed edgewise, as piling it makes it tough instead of crisp, as the steam cannot escape when piled.

It is particularly useful to know how to make delicate toast, for when it is nicely made it will tempt the appetite of any invalid. Professor Chandler has stated that bread is more healthful when toasted.

All of these things it is well to know, and that you may make the best use of your knowledge is the wish of your friend and teacher.

## LESSON FIRST.

QUESTIONS.

*Question. What is the nicest way of toasting?*
*Answer.* Before the fire—not over it.
*Q. How must toast be to be perfect?*
*A.* Crisp and tender, so that the cream will just lie on the outside of it, and not soak through it like a pudding.
*Q. How should the Toast Crumbs be served?*
*A.* In a dish by themselves, with a table-spoon to serve them.
*Q. How should the Rare-bit be served?*
*A.* The toast as the Milk Toast, with the dressing between the slices; the dressing will be thicker, and the *cheese* will make it look tougher.
*Q. How should the Water Toast be?*
*A.* Not too wet, and in an even pile.
*Q. In making any kind of gravy or cream for toast, Welsh Rarebit, etc., how must it be to be right?*
*A.* Smooth and free from lumps, and of the right thickness.
*Q. What thickness should the dressing be?*
*A.* About as thick as cream—not as thick as condensed milk.
*Q. What is used for thickening sauces and cream?*
*A.* Flour, corn-starch, and eggs.
*Q. How are they prepared?*
*A.* Flour is wet with a little cold water at first, and stirred free from lumps, then a little more water is added to make it thinner. Corn-starch is made in the same way, and when eggs are used for thickening they are beaten with white and yelk together. Butter and flour are sometimes rubbed together for sauce.
*Q. When should the thickening be added to the sauce?*
*A.* When the sauce is at the boiling-point, set the saucepan back from the fire, while adding the thickening, stirring constantly.
*Q. How long does it take to cook the thickening?*
*A.* Cook flour about five minutes. Corn-starch takes less time, and when eggs are used they need constant watching.
*Q. What will happen if you let thickening stand without stirring, or put it in when the sauce is too hot?*
*A.* It will be lumpy.

# RECEIPTS.

### MILK TOAST.

4 Slices of bread.
1 Pint of milk.
1 Table-spoon of flour.
½ Teaspoon of salt.
A little butter.

Cut bread in even slices one-third of an inch thick.. When toasted and buttered, lay in a deep dish and pour the thickened milk over it.

### WELSH RARE-BIT.

6 Slices of bread.
4 Table-spoons of grated cheese.
1 Pint of milk.
¼ Teaspoon of salt.
1 Egg.
½ Table-spoon of flour.

Cut bread in even slices, toast, and place on a platter. The milk should be ready for thickening when the toast is made. While thickening, add an egg well beaten, cheese, and salt; stir until the *cheese* melts, pour over the toast, and serve.

### QUEEN TOAST.

1 Pint of milk.
1 Egg.
1 Table-spoon each of lard, sugar, and butter; a little cinnamon.

Beat the egg, stir in the milk, lay the bread, cut in three-cornered pieces, to soak. Put butter and lard in frying-pan, and, when hot, fry the bread in this until brown on both sides. Serve with sugar and cinnamon sprinkled between the slices.

### WATER TOAST.

Cut bread in even slices, then toast; dip in boiling salted water.

Cut small bits of butter, and lay on each slice; when all are buttered singly, pile, and put in the oven for a few minutes.

### TOAST CRUMBS.

Cut even slices of stale bread; butter, and cut in dice; put them in a pan, buttered side up, and brown in the oven.

*Recapitulation of the Lesson.*

### MILK TOAST.

1 We cut our slices the same thickness to toast.
2 We put the milk into the saucepan.
3 We toast the bread.
4 We butter the toast, and keep it warm.
5 We put the milk over to heat.
6 We rub the butter and flour together.
7 We add the butter and flour, with the salt, to the milk, when the milk is heated near boiling.
8 We stir the milk until about as thick as cream.
9 We place the toast in a warm dish, dipping the hot cream over each slice.
Now it is finished.

### WELSH RARE-BIT.

1 We measure the milk, and put it over to heat.
2 We cut the bread in even slices.
3 We grate the cheese.
4 We beat the egg, yolk and white together.
5 We wet the flour with a little milk.
6 We toast the bread.
7 We pour the wet flour into the hot milk, and stir until it is cooked.
8 We pound the crust of the bread toast, and place it in a warm dish.
9 We add the beaten egg and cheese (grated) into the thickened milk.

## LESSON FIRST.

10 When the cheese is melted, dip the dressing over each slice of toast.

Now it is finished.

### QUEEN TOAST.

1 We cut our bread in moderately thick slices.
2 We beat our egg with a teaspoon of sugar.
3 We mix the milk and egg together.
4 We put our butter and lard in frying-pan to heat.
5 We mix two table-spoons of sugar with a salt-spoon of cinnamon.
6 We dip our slices of bread in the milk and egg.
7 We fry in hot butter on both sides until a light brown.
8 We place the slices in a pile on a hot dish, sprinkling sugar and cinnamon between the slices.

Now it is finished.

### WATER TOAST.

1 We cut the bread as for other toast.
2 We put over the spider half full of boiling water, with salt, and a little butter.
3 We butter our toasted bread.
4 We dip our buttered toast into the hot salted water.
5 We make a nice pile on a warm plate, and place in the oven.

Now it is finished.

### TOAST CRUMBS.

1 We cut the stale bread in moderately thick slices.
2 We spread the slices with butter.
3 We cut each slice into dice.
4 We place in a dripping-pan high in the oven.
5 We watch, and shake, to turn them.

When a light brown they are finished.

## LESSON FIRST.

## DIAGRAM OF TABLES.

```
TEACHER'S TABLE.

Flour. Salt, etc.        Dishes.
```

Frying-pan,
Grater, Bowl,
Fork. Cup, and Spoon,
Plate of Bread.

Table-spoon.
Toasting-fork,
Eggs and Cheese,
Plate of Butter.

Toasting-fork.
Table-spoon,
Frying-pan.

Pint Measure,
Teacup. Spoon,
Plate of Bread.

Saucepan and Fork,
Skimmer,
Plate of Bread,
Toasting-fork.

Plate of Butter.

Plate of Bread,
Two Baking-pans.

Bowl, Egg-beater,
Eggs, Frying-pan.

```
STOVE.

Kettle.
```

# LESSON SECOND.

"NOTHING BUT POTATOES."

# SECOND COOKING LESSON.

## BILL OF FARE.

MASHED POTATOES.

STEWED POTATOES.

FRIED POTATOES.

STUFFED POTATOES.

RICED POTATOES.

*Utensils Required.*

- 12 Table-boards.
- 12 Small Pans.
- 12 Paring-knives.
- 3 Towels or Napkins.
- 1 Dripping-pan.
- 1 Quart Bowl.
- 6 Forks.
- 18 Teaspoons.
- 1 Frying-pan and Cover.
- 1 Coarse Towel.
- 1 Skimmer.
- 1 Tin Saucepan and Cover.
- 1 Porcelain-lined Kettle and Cover.
- 1 Colander.
- 3 Vegetable-dishes.
- 1 Board to stand hot Kettles on.
- 6 Table-spoons.
- 1 Tin Pitcher.
- 2 Water-pails.
- 6 Knives.
- 1 Small Tin Saucepan.
- 2 Teacups.
- BELL.

MATERIAL REQUIRED—EXPENSE.

| | | |
|---|---|---|
| 22 | Medium-sized Potatoes | $0 12 |
| 1 | Pint of Milk | 04 |
| ¼ | Lb. of Butter | 13 |
| ¼ | Lb. of Lard | 04 |
| | Salt | 01 |
| | Pepper | 01 |
| | Flour | 01 |
| | | $0 36 |

# Order of Exercise.

### MARCH.

#### CHORD—BE SEATED.

Song—"*All we little Girls.*"

*Lecture.*

*A few Questions.*

*Read Bill of Fare.*

Appoint three girls to each receipt.
Start girls paring potatoes, and explain the way.
Teacher show samples of cutting potatoes.
Start all receipts, reserving stewed potatoes.
Last, stew potatoes.

*Questions*—10 *minutes.*

Fry potatoes and salt them.
Mash boiled potatoes.

Song—"*Salt Song.*"

Stuff baked potatoes.
Stew potatoes.

Song—"*Growing Potatoes.*"

#### CHORD—RISE, MARCH, EACH GIRL WITH HER OWN UTENSILS.

## LETTER ON POTATOES.

You are to have a lesson on the potato. This, you know, is the most common vegetable used in every family, therefore it is desirable to know something about its history, and the most appetizing and nutritious way of cooking it. Sir Walter Raleigh, one of the early explorers of this country, finding the potato, and realizing its value, tried to persuade people to cultivate it. Most people are very slow to try new things, so it was a long time before it came into common use.

It is said that Sir Walter Raleigh, at a court reception, wore a potato blossom in his button-hole, so as to call the attention of the company to the subject, and to secure their help in introducing it into England.

We are to have potatoes prepared in four ways, and I wish you each to learn all of these ways. So you must give attention to the different receipts, which are in plain sight for you to apply.

Those which you try here yourselves you will know how to do; you can also learn a little by seeing how the others prepare their part of the lesson.

It takes a great deal of practice to make a good cook, so you will have to try all the plans we give you in your homes, and if you do not succeed at first, do not be discouraged, but try again. I am very sure these lessons will be useful to you. Cooks are very necessary people, for one cannot have a very comfortable home who does not know how to make nice and inviting dishes.

People's tastes may vary in regard to cooking potatoes. Most persons in this country like them dry and mealy, like a ball of starch. The Irish think them best when boiled to leave their hearts a little hard- with a bone in it, they say.

The French use potatoes a great deal, but hardly ever have them plain boiled, but dress them in various ways.

The Germans like them as a salad.

Potatoes consist of about one-fifth starch, four-fifths water, gum, and other substances. They contain very little of the phosphates, which form a large part of the bones of the body.

The Irish supply this want by using a great deal of skim-milk and buttermilk with their potatoes. When people depend upon one kind of food, it is very important that it should do all that is needed to strengthen every part of the body; but we use a good many things besides potatoes.

I am anxious to have you learn all that you can about cooking the common dishes used in a family. There is no other vegetable you can cook in such a variety of ways as the potato. Since you cannot always judge how much will be eaten, and since nothing which is good should be wasted, I shall, after a while, give you a lesson on warmed-over potatoes.

When a dish is poor, a woman should know why it is so.

Boiled potatoes will be dark and waxy if after they are cooked they are allowed to remain in a covered kettle or dish, for the steam will return into the potato and bring about this condition. They will be floury and white if, after the moment they are cooked, all the water is drained off and the kettle is covered with a clean towel, through which the steam escapes.

Mashed potatoes will be hard and sticky and heavy if you turn cold milk upon them while they are steaming hot, but by adding scalding milk, and beating them thoroughly, they will be light and feathery. Until served, they should be covered close with a napkin.

Fried potatoes will be soaked and leathery if the fat is not hot enough, and if they are not well drained when taken out.

Later on in the lesson, one of the teachers will ask you a few questions about what I have told you, but now we will go at once to work, remembering all we taught in the last lesson.

## QUESTIONS.

*Question.* Which is the most common vegetable used?
*Answer.* Potato.
*Q.* Of what is it mostly formed?
*A.* Of starch.
*Q.* What is the simplest way of cooking it?
*A.* Boiling.
*Q.* How long does it take?
*A.* Thirty minutes from the beginning of boiling.
*Q.* What part is thrown away?
*A.* The skin.
*Q.* What effect does soaking in water have upon them?
*A.* It swells them, and also freshens them.
*Q.* How can boiled potatoes wait without harm?
*A.* Covered with a thin towel.
*Q.* How should they be served whole?
*A.* Laid in a dish on a napkin, and covered with the fringed corners.
*Q.* How do you know when an oven is hot?
*A.* When the oven door hisses, or flour will brown in five minutes.
*Q.* How do you know when water boils in a kettle?
*A.* When the steam puffs out of the spout.
*Q.* How do you know when water boils in a saucepan?
*A.* When it bubbles all over.
*Q.* How do you know when fat is hot enough to boil in?
*A.* When the smoke rises from the centre.
*Q.* Which is hottest when it boils, water or fat?
*A.* Fat.
*Q.* What must you remember in stewing with milk?
*A.* That it burns easily.
*Q.* How long must potatoes bake?
*A.* About 45 minutes—a medium-sized potato in an ordinary oven.

*Q. How long will it take to fry potatoes?*
*A.* Ten minutes, watching all the time.
*Q. How long does it take to stew potatoes?*
*A.* About 30 minutes for uncooked potatoes.
*Q. When do you salt boiled potatoes?*
*A.* When you start to boil them.
*Q. How much salt?*
*A.* About half a table-spoonful to a quart of water.

# RECEIPTS.

### MASHED POTATOES.

Pare and plain boil, mash in the same vessel in which they are cooked, and season with hot milk, butter, and salt to taste; beat with a fork, and arrange neatly in a hot dish, or glaze over with butter, and brown in the oven. If browned, cut across each way, that the crust may not bind.

### STEWED POTATOES.

Cover in salted boiling water (after paring); when nearly soft, drain and cover with same quantity of milk; when it boils, thicken with flour, and season.

### FRIED POTATOES.

Pare and cut in strips as nearly the same size as possible. When the fat is hot, dry the potatoes in a clean towel and put in enough to float over the top of the fat. Take them up with a skimmer and place on brown paper. Salt just before serving.

### STUFFED POTATOES.

Cut one end of the potato so that it will stand steady; cut the other almost off like a little cover. Put them in a pan and bake; when soft, take the potato from the shell with a fork very carefully; mix with butter and salt, and about three table-spoonfuls of hot milk; beat well, and fill the shells heaping full; put high in the oven to brown.

### RICED POTATOES.

Pare, plain boil, mash, and season with salt; rub with a wooden spoon through a hot colander; put low in the oven to heat, but not brown.

## LESSON SECOND.

*Recapitulation of the Lesson.*

#### MASHED POTATOES.

1 We pare and drop into cold water.
2 We put on to cook in salted boiling water.
3 They boil about thirty minutes.
4 We drain the water off.
5 We mash the potato in the kettle in which it has been boiled.
6 We put in hot milk, butter, more salt if needed, and beat with a fork.
7 We arrange neatly in a hot dish.

#### STEWED POTATOES.

1 We wash, pare, and drop into cold water.
2 We cut in small squares and drop them into another bowl of cold water.
3 We drain them, and put into an iron frying-pan.
4 We turn in boiling water enough to cover them, sprinkle with salt, and put over to boil.
5 We rub one teaspoonful of butter and flour together.
6 We wash and cut a little parsley very fine.
7 We turn off the water when the potatoes are nearly soft, and turn on milk to cover them.
8 When milk boils, we stir in butter and flour.
9 We let them boil, stirring carefully till the milk is creamy.
10 We toss in the parsley as we take the potatoes from the stove, and turn in a hot dish for serving.
Now it is finished.

#### FRIED POTATOES.

1 We put lard on to heat.
2 We wash and pare potatoes, and drop into cold water.
3 We quarter lengthwise, then divide in even strips, and drop into cold water.
4 We test the heat of the lard with one piece of potato.
5 We dry in a clean towel enough potatoes to fry at one time.
6 We stand by and stir gently with a skimmer.

7 We drain them with a skimmer against the side of the kettle.

8 We take them out, drop them on brown paper, and sprinkle with salt.

Now, when all are thus cooked, we are finished.

### STUFFED POTATOES.

1 We wash and scrub the skins.

2 We cut one end of the potato so that it will stand upright.

3 We cut the other end like a cover, making all the potatoes of one height.

4 We stand them in the dripping-pan, and place in the oven to bake. (They should bake until soft.)

5 We take the dripping-pan from the oven and stand it on a piece of brown paper on the table.

6 We put a cup of milk to heat.

7 We hold the baked potato with a dish-towel in one hand, and a fork in the other.

8 We carefully take out the potato in a bowl, and place the empty shells in a pan.

9 We gradually add hot milk, butter and salt, and beat until light.

10 We fill the shells with the mixture with a fork as high as we can.

11 We place high in the oven to brown.

12 When a light brown, we place on a hot dish to serve.

Now it is finished.

### RICED POTATOES.

1 We cook as for mashed potatoes.

2 We heat the colander.

3 We mash the potatoes in the kettle in which they have been boiled.

4 We taste, and if needed we add salt.

5 We heat the dish in which the potato is to be served.

6 We place the hot colander over the hot dish, and stir the potato rapidly through with a wooden spoon.

Now it is finished.

## LESSON SECOND.

### DIAGRAM OF TABLES.

|  | TEACHER'S TABLE. |  |
|---|---|---|
|  | Moulding-board. |  |
| Butter, Lard, Water, Milk, Salt, Flour. | Board for Hot Plates | Vegetable-dishes, Tasting-spoon. |

Table 1 (left):
① 
② Six Potatoes, Dripping-pan, Bowl, Three Forks.
③
③ Four Potatoes, Frying-pan and Cover, Cup and Spoon, Salt-shaker, Fork.
② ①

Table 2 (right):
①
② Four Potatoes, Fork, Saucepan and Cover, Colander, Bowl, Masher.
③
③ Two Potatoes, Porcelain Kettle, Skimmer, Salt-shaker, Plate and Paper.
② ①

STOVE.

Kettle.

# LESSON THIRD.

# THIRD COOKING LESSON.

## BILL OF FARE.

SCRAMBLED EGGS.

BAKED OMELET.

POACHED EGGS.

QUAKER OMELET.

PLAIN OMELET.

### *Utensils Required.*

- 3 Frying-pans.
- 1 Baking-dish.
- 1 Skimmer.
- 1 Toasting-fork.
- 8 Teacups.
- 2 Bowls.

- 3 Forks.
- 4 Table-spoons.
- 3 Teaspoons.
- 1 Broad Knife.
- 1 Platter to beat whites of eggs.

### MATERIAL REQUIRED—EXPENSE.

| | |
|---|---|
| 1 Dozen Eggs | $0 35 |
| 1 Pint of Milk | 04 |
| ¼ Lb. of Butter | 12 |
| 3 Pieces of Stale Bread | |
| Salt, Pepper | 01 |
| Flour | 01 |
| | $0 53 |

# Order of Exercise.

### MARCH.

#### CHORD—BE SEATED.

Song—*"Beating Eggs."*

*Lecture.*

*A few Questions.*

*Read Bill of Fare.*

Appoint three girls to each receipt.

Have the eggs to be poached dropped carefully into separate cups.

The eggs to be scrambled, or made into omelet, have broken in such a way as to drop the yolks and whites into different dishes.

For the omelet have yolks and whites beaten separately.

For the scrambled eggs, yolks and whites can be beaten together, but for practice have them separated when broken.

Have toast made for poached eggs.

Then have eggs poached, and eggs to be *baked put in oven.*

Next the scrambled eggs should be cooked—*lastly, the omelet.*

When all is cooked, have girls taste.

*Review Questions.*

*Dismiss Class.*

## A LETTER ON EGGS.

Our lesson to-day is on eggs. They are very nutritious, and, like milk, contain all the material necessary for the growth of the body. They are composed of two distinct substances.

The yolk contains nearly one-third of its weight in oil.

The white, or albumen, is the same as the gluten in meats.

There is also a large part of sulphur and other mineral matters.

The sulphur gives the egg its yellow color, and it is this which causes the egg to tarnish silver. The most healthful ways of cooking eggs are boiling, poaching, and in omelets.

The common mode of putting the eggs into boiling water, and letting them boil rapidly for two or three minutes, is not the best way, as the heat hardens the albumen near the shell, and in this way, while the white of the egg becomes very hard, the yolk has not begun to cook. The better way, when they are wanted very soft, is to pour boiling water on them, cover closely, and let them stand where they will keep hot, but not boil, for ten minutes.

Another way is to put them on in cold water, and let them come to a boil, which will be in ten minutes; but if you want a *hard* boiled egg, put it on in the same way and let it remain for half an hour.

If they are to be used for garnishing, when boiled, lay them in cold water to prevent the yolk from turning dark.

Heat cooks our food, and beating eggs rapidly makes them very warm, so that when the white of an egg is thoroughly beaten it is partially cooked.

A raw egg digests more easily than a cooked egg.

Throwing the white of the egg into the air with long strokes causes little air-cells or bubbles to be formed. These can be broken down by striking or by weight.

If you are making the top for a pudding, and pour the sugar upon the beaten egg, many of these air-cells will be broken, but if, on the contrary, you pour it at one end of the dish, and beat it in little by little, by drawing it under the egg, your frosting will be much lighter.

If you are making a custard, and wish the egg to thicken the milk, if you separate the yolk and white, and fill the white with air, it will be lighter than the milk and float on the top, and so leave the milk as thin as ever.

In most kinds of cakes the whites and yolks are beaten separately; in such cases the whites are beaten in last, or with a part of the flour.

There is oil in the yolk; this makes the cake richer, and cake made of the yolk and white will not dry as fast as that made entirely of the whites.

While eggs are nourishing, they are not so heating to the blood as meat, and doctors often order them for patients who need nourishment and yet cannot have their blood heated by meat juices.

To learn how to cook them delicately and nicely is almost an art, and, although you will be shown but a few ways of cooking eggs in this lesson, it will be a guide in breaking, beating, and arranging eggs by other receipts.

While eggs are cheaper in the spring I hope you will try to cook them, although when they cost the most you can really get more nourishment from them than for the same amount of money spent for meat.

---

QUESTIONS.

*Question. What do physicians say of eggs?*

*Answer.* They are very nutritious and less heating to the blood than meat.

*Q. Of what is the egg composed?*
*A.* Yolk and white.

*Q. What part of the yolk is oil?*
*A.* One-third of its weight.

*Q. What is the white, or albumen, the same as?*
*A.* The gluten in meat.

*Q. Why does the egg tarnish silver?*
*A.* Because the yolk contains sulphur.

*Q. What other way is there of boiling eggs besides letting them boil rapidly for three or four minutes?*

*A.* If they are to be *soft*, pour boiling water on them, cover closely, and keep hot, but not boil, for ten minutes.

*Q. Mention another way?*

*A.* Put them on in cold water and let it come to a boil in ten minutes.

*Q. If they are wanted very hard, how would you boil them?*

*A.* Put them on in cold water and let them boil thirty minutes.

*Q. When eggs are to be used for garnishing, what should you do with them to prevent the yolk from turning a dark color?*

*A.* When boiled, lay them in cold water.

*Q. Which digests more quickly, a raw or a cooked egg?*

*A.* A raw egg.

*Q. How should you beat an egg?*

*A.* With long strokes, throwing the white into the air.

*Q. In mixing frosting for cake or pudding, how should you mix the sugar with the beaten whites?*

*A.* Turn the sugar in at one end of the dish, and beat it in little by little, drawing it under the eggs.

*Q. What kind of cake keeps the best?*

*A.* That in which the *yolks* as well as the *whites* are used.

*Q. Which are the four ways in which we have learned to cook eggs?*

*A.* Scrambled, Baked Omelet, Poached Eggs, and Quaker Omelet.

# RECEIPTS.

### SCRAMBLED EGGS.

Three eggs, one-half cup of milk, one teaspoonful of butter and flour each, salt-spoonful of salt. Heat and thicken the milk, add butter and salt, then stir in the eggs. Turn into a hot dish.

### BAKED OMELET.

One scant pint of milk, two eggs, one-half table-spoonful of butter and flour each, one-half teaspoonful of salt. Let the milk come to a boil. Mix butter and flour together; stir it into the milk. Let it cool five minutes, stirring constantly. Put it where it will cool. When *cool*, add the salt and eggs (eggs beaten separately); pour into a buttered dish. Bake twenty minutes in a quick oven. Serve at once.

### POACHED EGGS.

Have salted boiling water in the frying-pan. Drop each egg in separately. When the white is set, baste. With a skimmer remove each egg and serve on buttered toast.

### QUAKER OMELET.

Three eggs, one-half cup of milk, one table-spoonful of butter, one and one-half table-spoonfuls of corn-starch, one teaspoonful of salt. Put the saucepan on to heat. Beat the yolks of the eggs, and stir smoothly the corn-starch into the milk, and add to the beaten yolks, also salt. Put butter into the hot pan (before putting butter beat the whites to a stiff froth and add to the yolks and milk), then when butter is melted pour in the mixture, *cover*, and place on the stove where it will brown but not burn. Cook about seven minutes. Fold and turn on a hot dish.

Plain Omelet the same as Quaker Omelet, only leave out the flour.

## LESSON THIRD.

*Recapitulation of the Lesson.*

### SCRAMBLED EGGS.

1 We put the milk on to heat.
2 We wet the flour with a little milk.
3 We add the butter and salt.
4 We break and beat the eggs, and stir them into the hot milk.
5 We keep stirring until sufficiently thick.
Now it is finished.

### BAKED OMELET.

1 We measure and put the milk to heat.
2 We stir the flour and butter together.
3 We wet it smooth with a little of the milk.
4 When the milk boils we pour it on this mixture.
5 We stand by and stir five minutes.
6 We put it away to cool.
7 We break the eggs separately.
8 We beat the whites well.
9 We pour the whites into the yolks and beat together.
10 We add the salt to the milk and eggs.
11 We put into a well-buttered dish and bake twenty minutes.
Now it is finished.

### POACHED EGGS.

1 We cut the bread in pieces half an inch thick, and near the size of the egg when cooked.
2 We toast and butter the bread.
3 We fill the frying-pan with boiling water, and add one teaspoonful of salt.
4 We knock an egg against the side of a cup and break it.
5 We let each egg stand in its own cup.
6 We draw the saucepan where the water will not boil fast.
7 We slip in one egg.
8 When the white is set slip in another.
9 With a spoon we baste the egg with the boiling water.
10 We baste till a white veil comes over the yolks.

11 Now the eggs are cooked, remove with a skimmer, and place an egg on each piece of toast.

Now they are finished.

### QUAKER OMELET.

1  We stir the milk gradually on the flour.
2  We put the frying-pan on to warm.
3  We break the eggs, separating yolks and whites.
4  We beat them so that the whites will stand alone and the yolks are well beaten.
5  We add the milk, flour, and salt to the beaten yolks.
6  We put the butter in the frying-pan.
7  We beat the whites quickly into the other mixture and turn it into the frying-pan.
8  We lift the edge with a knife to see if it is brown.
9  We set it in the oven for a moment to cook the middle.
10  We fold it over.
11  We turn it on a hot platter and serve immediately.

## LESSON THIRD.

### DIAGRAM OF TABLES.

```
┌─────────────────────────────────────────────┐
│            TEACHER'S TABLE.                 │
│                                             │
│   Milk,      Eggs,         Extra Spoons.    │
│   Flour.     Butter,       Necessary Dishes.│
│              Bread.                         │
└─────────────────────────────────────────────┘
```

┌───────────────────────┐    ┌───────────────────────┐
│         | ○           │    │         |○            │
│  ○                    │    │                    ○  │
│ ―  Bowl, Fork,        │    │  Frying-pan,          │
│    Platter, Fork,     │    │  Skimmer,             │
│    Teacup and Spoon,  │    │  Three Teacups,       │
│    Frying-pan,        │    │  Toasting-fork.       │
│    Bread-knife.       │    │                       │
│                       │    │                    ○  │
│  ○                    │    │                       │
│                       │    │                       │
│                       │    │                    ○  │
│  ○                    │    │                       │
│                       │    │  Teaspoon,            │
│    Two Bowls,         │    │  Three Teacups,       │
│    Frying-pan,        │    │  Baking Platter.      │
│    Table-spoon,       │    │                    ○  │
│    Teacup and Spoon.  │    │                       │
│  ○                    │    │       ○|              │
│         ○|            │    │                       │
└───────────────────────┘    └───────────────────────┘

```
        ┌─────────────┐
        │   STOVE.    │
        └─────────────┘
```

# LESSON FOURTH.

"LET US HASTE ON,

MARKET DAY."

IT IS MARKET DAY,

# FOURTH COOKING LESSON.

## BILL OF FARE.

ROAST BEEF.

FRIED STEAK.

MOCK DUCK.

BROILED STEAK.

BREADED CHOPS.

### *Utensils Required.*

| | |
|---|---|
| 12 Table-boards. | 1 Gridiron. |
| 12 Knives. | 1 Spider. |
| 3 Forks. | 4 Meat-platters. |
| 6 Table-spoons. | 1 Small Gravy-bowl. |
| 6 Teaspoons. | 4 Plates for Meat. |
| 1 Teacup. | 1 Dripping-pan and Rack. |
| 2 Bowls. | 2 Flat Plates, one for beaten egg, |
| 2 Saucepans. | and one for cracker-dust. |
| 3 Small Pans. | Dredging-boxes. |

### MATERIAL REQUIRED—EXPENSE.

Beef to roast, off the round.  
2 Steaks.  
1 Flank of Beef.  
6 Potatoes.  

¼ lb. of Butter.  
Flour.  
Salt and Pepper.  
2 Bowls of cold Water.

| | |
|---|---:|
| Roast of Beef | $0 24 |
| Steaks | 22 |
| Flank of Beef | 30 |
| Potatoes | 03 |
| Flour, Salt, Pepper, and Butter | 06 |
| | $0 85 |

# Order of Exercise.

### MARCH.

### CHORD—BE SEATED.

### Song—"*Meat Song.*"

### *Lecture.*

### *A few Questions.*

### Song—"*Marketing Song.*"

### *Read Bill of Fare.*

Appoint three girls to each receipt.
Start all girls preparing meat for being cooked.
When the roast is dredged with salt and flour, place in oven.
Have the girls prepare the flank for mock duck.
Have girls who are to broil steak pare potatoes, and attend to the boiling of them.
When potatoes are partially boiled, drain and place on rack with roast.
Broil steak when the fire is hot and clear.
Heat frying-pan for dry fry when roast is almost done.
Appoint one girl to prepare thickening for roast-beef gravy.
Appoint two other girls for preparing hot platters for steaks, with butter, salt, and pepper on them.
The girls who are roasting beef have hot platters ready when meal is prepared, class be seated, and teacher give each a portion to taste.

# LETTER ON MEATS.

Your lessons about meat will, I hope, be both useful and interesting to you.

I want to give you a few hints about cooking it, and afterward you will receive directions about buying it.

There are light and dark meats. The dark must be cooked rare, so that in carving the juice will follow the knife. As a general rule, the light must be cooked thoroughly.

However it is cooked, it must always be prepared in the same way.

Except for soup, the juices must be kept inside the meat.

There is a gummy substance in meat that can be hardened by great heat, and made to form a crust on the outside, shutting in all the juices. It is something like the white of an egg, when hardened by heat it encloses the yolk.

However meat is cooked, this crust must form on the outside. To produce this result, it must be exposed at first to a great heat, but cooked more slowly toward the last.

Meat cooked rapidly will be hard all the way through.

*To roast*, your oven should be very hot at first, then slow and steady.

*To boil*, the water must be boiling at first, then simmer gently.

*To fry*, the smoke must rise from the centre of the pan, to show it is hot enough.

*To broil*, the fire must be so hot that the outside of your meat is seared at once.

The meats upon which we mostly depend are beef from the ox and cow, mutton and lamb from the sheep, pork from the pig, and veal from the calf.

Ox beef is much nicer than cow beef, and you can know it by the color, which is a dark red, well mingled with fat, of a rich white shade, and a fine grain.

Cow beef is paler, and much firmer.

Lamb is more delicate than mutton.

## LESSON FOURTH.

Pork and veal are not considered so healthful as beef or lamb, though both make delicious dishes.

The fat in beef is very valuable in cooking, but the fat of lamb or mutton should not be mingled with other dishes on account of its strong flavor.

From pork we get our best lard, and salt pork is excellent for seasoning other meats, and makes a nice dish fried in thin stripes.

To cook salt meats which have been prepared for winter use, or to be used on long sea voyages, place them in *cold* water first, to draw out the salt, and then allow them slowly to come to a boil.

Ham is much nicer if the skin is removed before boiling, as it has a strong, smoky taste.

Many of these things you can only learn by experience.

After this lesson, if you give good attention, you will know how to cook any ordinary roast, to broil or fry a steak, or cook a piece of corned beef.

After your chart lesson you will better understand how to buy meat to advantage.

When you have learned all these things, and have seen how much better it is to make proper use of your material, if you try your skill at home, nothing would be more gratifying to me than to know you are profiting by my teaching.

### CHART LESSON.

In this chart lesson I take the ox, which is the most important animal.

The *skin* is made into leather, the *hair* is used to strengthen mortar, and the *horns* and *hoofs* are made into handles for knives and forks.

The *tongue* is cooked, and the *tail* makes excellent soup.

When the animal is brought to market it is cut into quarters, called the fore-quarters and the hind-quarters.

In the hind-quarters there is a large bone called the whirl-bone, by which the butchers twist the leg, and straighten it out as you see it hung in the market by the shank. At the other end of this piece of meat the porter-house steak begins, and the rib, or prime roast, is found in the fore-quarter where it joins the hind-quarter.

While feeding or walking the ox constantly moves its head and legs, so that in these parts the blood runs more actively, and the circulation makes the flesh firmer and the muscles stronger. These parts are therefore *tougher*, but really contain the most nourishment.

Where the body is at rest the meat is more tender.

The best sirloin steaks are near the porter-house, and are more economical. The *sirloin* is also very nice for roasting.

The *rump* is used for corning, and the *round* for steaks, and especially for beef-tea, as it is very juicy.

The thin flank can be used to make a very nice dish called "Mock Duck."

The thick flank is often corned.

The chuck is tough but very nutritious.

As only one-sixth of the ox is tender, we must learn to cook the rest in a way to make it so also.

QUESTIONS ON MEATS.

*Q. How should you prepare meat for cooking?*
*A.* Scrape and trim your piece of meat,
Then with wet cloth wipe it neat;
When it is cut but slightly wet it,
Nor in a bowl of water set it.

*Q. What are the ordinary ways of cooking?*
*A.* Roast, boil, fry, and broil.

*Q. How can you shut the juices in?*
*A.* A crust must form on the outside,
And close within the juices hide;
Unless at first great heat you try,
The juice will go, and leave it dry.

*Q. How do you boil?*
*A.* Be sure the water is boiling hot
Before you plunge the meat in the pot;
And for ten minutes keep it so,
Then set it back and cook it slow.

## LESSON FOURTH.

*Q. How do you broil?*
*A.* The fire must be so hot and clear,
The meat outside to quickly sear;
So do not leave it on the fire—
Stand near and turn it, do not tire.

*Q. How do you roast?*
*A.* First put your rack into the pan,
Dredge the roast lightly as you can;
First use the salt, and generous be,
Then shake the flour, with both be free;
Your oven now must have such power,
Five minutes sure must brown the flour;
That on the pan will cook and lie
To make the gravy by and by.
Now water, half an inch or so,
Turn in one end, and let it flow
Over the surface of the pan,
But touch the meat it never can.
Often turn the roast from side to side,
For all the juices you must hide
Within a crust so crisp and light,
Frothy and brown, a tempting sight.
Now an important time has come—
Cook slowly till the meat is done,
And every fifteen minutes baste it,
First gravy, salt, and flour to paste it.

*Q. What about gravies?*
*A.* Gravies, sauces, soups must be
Smooth and free from fat to see;
None should be more thick than cream—
Some so clear, the spoon is seen.

### MARKETING QUESTIONS.

*Q. What is beef?*
*A.* Ox or cow meat?
*Q. Which is the better?*
*A.* The ox.

## LESSON FOURTH.

*Q. How can you tell the difference?*
*A.* Ox meat is red, well mingled with fat, and of a fine grain; while cow beef is paler and of a firmer grain.
*Q. Of what color should the fat be?*
*A.* A clear, rich white, tinged with yellow.
*Q. How can you tell good beef?*
*A.* When you press it with your finger and the meat rises quickly.
*Q. How is the beef cut at the market?*
*A.* Into four quarters.
*Q. What are the best roasting-pieces?*
*A.* Sirloin and middle ribs.
*Q. What are the most economical steaks?*
*A.* Sirloin or round.
*Q. How do you know the round steaks?*
*A.* The fat lies on the top.
*Q. What is the most tender steak?*
*A.* The porter-house.
*Q. Where is it found?*
*A.* Between the rib and the sirloin.
*Q. How much of the ox is tough?*
*A.* Five-sixths.
*Q. What can be done with tough parts?*
*A.* Corn the rump, and use other parts for stews, pot-roasts, and mince-pie meat.
*Q. What parts are used for soups?*
*A.* The leg, shank, tail, and neck.

# RECEIPTS.

### TO ROAST MEAT.

Prepare as directed, place on rack in the pan, dredging well, first with salt and then with flour.

When flour is brown, pour boiling water in the pan about an inch deep. Baste and dredge frequently. When done, place the meat on a heated platter; skim all fat from the pan, set it on the stove, and let it come to a boil; stir in thickening, and boil again.

### TO FRY STEAK.

Heat frying-pan very hot, then sprinkle with salt and lay in steak, having first cut fat in two or three places to prevent meat from curling; turn it often.

When done, remove to a hot platter; pour a little boiling water into the pan, and this will, with the juice, make a nice gravy to pour over the meat.

### MOCK DUCK.

Trim a piece of thin flank. Prepare a dressing, as for turkey, of bread-crumbs, butter, salt, pepper, and onion chopped fine. Spread this over meat, and roll like jelly-cake. Tie it in the form of a duck, place it in a saucepan with boiling water about two inches deep; add a little water, if necessary as water boils away.

When tender and brown, take it out upon a platter and turn gravy over it, or serve separately.

### TO BROIL STEAK.

Warm the gridiron, on which place the steak, and hold over clear, hot coals; turn frequently till done. Serve on hot platter, buttered and seasoned.

### BREADED CHOPS.

Cleanse and trim them, slightly cook, and then dip each into beaten egg and seasoned cracker-dust, or fine bread-crumbs. Fry in hot lard or dripping.

*Recapitulation of the Lesson.*

#### ROAST MEAT.

1 We scrape and trim the meat.
2 We wipe it carefully with a wet cloth.
3 We place it on a rack in the pan.
4 We dredge it with salt and then with flour, shaking well on the pan.
5 We put it into a hot oven.
6 When the flour in the pan is brown we turn in hot water to cover the pan one-half inch.
7 We baste the meat with the hot water, and dredge again with flour and salt.
8 We turn the meat, and baste and dredge again.
9 We now cook slowly, twenty minutes to a pound.
10 When cooked, place on a hot dish, and it is finished.

#### FRIED STEAK.

1 We put the frying-pan on to heat.
2 We prepare the meat as for broiling.
3 We sprinkle salt over the hot frying-pan, and put in the meat.
4 We stand by and turn it often.
5 We place it on a hot platter, where butter is awaiting it.
6 We turn a very little hot water into the frying-pan, and pour it over the meat.
Now it is finished.

#### MOCK DUCK.

1 Trim and prepare the meat as for other cooking.
2 We crumb a small quantity of bread.
3 We chop half an onion.
4 We add bread to the onion in chopping-tray.

5 We add a good table-spoonful of butter.
6 We add two salt-spoonfuls of salt and one of pepper.
7 We mix together.
8 We place evenly on the meat.
9 We roll the meat like a roll of jelly-cake.
10 We make it smaller at the ends, shaping like a duck.
11 We sew it up, and tie it at the ends.
12 We place it in a kettle.
13 We turn in water to cover the meat two or three inches.
14 We add water as it boils away.
15 As the meat grows tender, let the water boil away and the meat brown.
16 We place on a hot platter, and turn gravy over it.

### BROILED STEAK.

1 We prepare the meat as for roasting.
2 We heat the gridiron.
3 We put the meat on the gridiron, with the fat toward the handle.
4 We stand by and hold the gridiron slanting over the coals.
5 We turn it often from side to side.
6 We place the meat on a hot platter, where butter, pepper, and a little salt are awaiting it.
7 We turn it, and press the butter and salt into it.
8 We cover with a hot cover, or platter, to draw the juices to the top.
Now it is finished.

### BREADED CHOPS.

1 We cleanse and trim them.
2 We place on a hot frying-pan and turn them once.
3 We take them out on a hot platter.
4 We break an egg and beat it.
5 We season some cracker-dust or bread-crumbs.
6 We dip each chop into the egg.
7 We dip them into the cracker-dust.
8 We fry in hot lard or dripping.
Now they are finished

## LESSON FOURTH.

### GRAVY.

1. If the drippings are too greasy skim off some of the fat.
2. We place the pan on the stove.
3. We turn in more boiling water.
4. We wet a table-spoonful of flour for the skimming.
5. We stir it into the gravy in the pan when it boils.
6. We taste, and if it is cooked it is finished.

## LESSON FOURTH.

### DIAGRAM OF TABLES.

TEACHER'S TABLE.

Water, Meat,
Flour, Butter,         Necessary Dishes.
Salt.

Saucepan.

Gridiron,
Saucepan,
Table-spoon.

Bowl of Water,
Towel.

Bowl of Water,
Towel.

Two Table-spoons,
Spider,
Dredging-box of Salt.

Dredging-boxes,
Salt and Pepper,
Teacup and Spoon,
Dripping-pan and Rack,
Two Table-spoons.

STOVE.

Kettle.

# LESSON FIFTH.

## FIFTH COOKING LESSON.

### BILL OF FARE.

CORN-BEEF HASH.

HASH ON TOAST.

WARMED-OVER MEATS.

MEAT ESCALOPED.

CROQUETS.

*Utensils Required.*

- 12 Boards.
- 12 Knives.
- 6 Forks.
- 4 Table-spoons.
- 1 Teacup.
- 3 Platters.
- 2 Chopping-bowls.
- 2 Chopping-knives.
- 2 Toasting-forks.

- 1 Baking-dish.
- 1 Mixing-bowl.
- 3 Frying-pans.
- 3 Small Pans.
- 1 Saucepan.
- 1 Pint Measure.
- 1 Strainer.
- 1 Dredging-box.
- 1 Towel.

### MATERIAL REQUIRED.

- 1¼ Lbs. of Corned Beef (ready cooked).
- 1 Small Steak " "
- 1 or 2 Lbs. of Stewing Beef (cooked and partly chopped).
- 6 Uncooked Potatoes.
- 6 Cold Boiled Potatoes.
- 4 Slices of Bread.
- ¼ Lb. of Butter.
- ½ Table-spoonful of Lard.
- ½ Pint of Milk.
- ½ Onion.
- Salt, Pepper, and Flour

## LESSON FIFTH.

### EXPENSE OF LESSON.

| | |
|---|---:|
| Corned Beef | $0 12 |
| Steak | 15 |
| Stewing Meat | 10 |
| Butter | 12 |
| Onion | 01 |
| Lard, Pepper, Salt, and Flour | 05 |
| | $0 55 |

# Order of Exercise.

### MARCH.

#### CHORD—BE SEATED.

Song—" *Meat Song.*"

*Lecture.*

*A few Questions.*

*Read Bill of Fare.*

Appoint three girls to each receipt.
Start the girls paring potatoes, and have them put on to boil as quickly as possible
Those making the warmed-over beefsteak cut onion, trim steak, and put on stove in frying-pan.
Set two girls to toast bread.
The remaining girls to chopping meat and potatoes.
Another girl to make thickening for beefsteak gravy.
One girl to cut steak in small pieces across the grain.
While steak is being cut, have gravy strained and thickened.
The girls who boiled potatoes, mash and season, and arrange in a dish.
When all the meat is cooking, those not busy be seated.
Taste the different dishes when prepared.

*Dismiss class after marketing song.*

## LETTER ON WARMED-OVER MEATS.

This lesson is about warmed-over meats, and it is very important to know how to cook them so that they will be appetizing.

Most people enjoy the various kinds of hashes if they are nicely prepared.

The richest are made of equal quantities of meat and potatoes; but this is not necessary, and the proportions can be varied as convenient.

Before the meat is chopped, cut away all bone and gristle; of these gravy can be made.

If the potatoes used for hash are cold, chop them; if freshly boiled, mash them.

When the hash is mixed and seasoned, it should be placed in a hot frying-pan, with a little lard to prevent it sticking. It should not be stirred, but allowed to brown, when it may be turned out flat on a platter, or doubled like an omelet.

Any kind of hash may be served in a dainty manner by placing it upon triangular pieces of toast, with the points turning toward the edge of the dish.

While chopping meat for hash without potatoes, dredge in a little flour. This will thicken it in cooking, and give it a richer flavor. Add salt while chopping, to season the meat.

It is better to add the pepper after it has been taken from the fire, as in cooking it loses its fresh and spicy taste.

The best cooks are careful to use freshly ground pepper, as it is not so good after it has been exposed to the air.

The excellence of food depends greatly upon its being properly seasoned.

Europeans ridicule American cooking, which they say is destitute of seasoning.

We, however, who have not been accustomed to it, would perhaps like their cooking no better.

The French are leaders of the civilized world in cooking as well as dressing.

## LESSON FIFTH.

When seasoning is perfect, no one flavor predominates over another. When using the onion for flavoring, great care should be taken to prevent it from being too noticeable. A few drops squeezed from the bulb is quite sufficient for hashes, soups, etc.

Gravies may be made for warmed-over meats by taking the fat trimmings from roasting-pieces and steaks, and trying them out, as it is called. Add water and a bit of onion, strain and thicken. When seasoned add the cut meat, but do not let it boil, as it toughens it.

All of these are good ways for using bits of meat, as well as economical. Sick people should be served with freshly cooked meats.

### QUESTIONS ON WARMED-OVER MEATS.

*Q. Is it necessary that all the meat should be of one kind for hash?*

*A.* No; but it must be chopped very fine.

*Q. How much potato should be used when mixed with meat?*

*A.* Usually the same quantity. A little more potato makes a plain hash.

*Q. How should meat be seasoned when mixed with potato?*

*A.* Dredge with salt and flour once or twice while chopping. Put in the frying-pan with a little water to moisten, and a bit of butter if meat is lean.

*Q. When must pepper be added?*

*A.* When you take it from the stove?

*Q. How can gravy be made for warmed-over meat?*

*A.* The bones and trimmings can be placed in a frying-pan, with a little chopped onion, some small bits of salt pork, and browned to color the gravy. Turn in boiling water, strain it, and thicken with flour.

*Q. How should toast be prepared when served under hash?*

*A.* The pieces should be of one size and shape, all crust removed, and browned nicely.

# RECEIPTS.

### CORN BEEF HASH.

To one pint of finely chopped beef add one pint of cold, boiled potatoes, also chopped, and two-thirds of a cup of hot water. Season with pepper and salt. Put a table-spoonful of butter or lard on a hot pan. Spread the hash smoothly, and cook slowly. When brown, turn into a hot platter, or fold over double like an omelet.

### HASH ON TOAST.

Chop meat fine, and dredge once or twice with flour. Add pepper and salt. Put it into frying-pan with a little butter and water to moisten it. Do not brown. Arrange slices of toast on platter, and turn hash over them.

### WARMED-OVER MEAT.

Make a gravy of bones and trimmings, a little onion or slice of salt pork. When brown, add a little hot water; salt and strain. Return to the pan and thicken with flour. Cut the meat across the grain into small pieces, stew thoroughly, but do not boil it. Sprinkle on pepper and salt.

### MEAT ESCALOPED.

Chop cold beef fine, and season. If you have no gravy, moisten with hot water and add a little butter. Put it into a baking-pan and cover with mashed potatoes. Glaze the top with butter, and before putting it in the oven gash the top to let out the steam. Brown nicely.

*Recapitulation of the Lesson.*

### CORN BEEF HASH.

1 We cut the meat into the tray, trimming off all the gristle and bits of skin.

2 We chop it very fine, chopping across the tray.
3 We turn it into a dish, and put potatoes into the tray.
4 We chop the potatoes
5 We put the frying-pan on to heat.
6 We turn the meat into the tray with the potatoes, and season it.
7 We add a little hot water slowly till sufficiently moist.
8 We put the butter in the frying-pan.
9 We spread in the hash.
10 We lift the hash with a broad knife to see if it is brown.
11 We sprinkle in a little pepper, if brown.
12 We fold it like an omelet.
Now it is finished.

### HASH ON TOAST.

1 We cut the meat in pieces into the tray and trim off the gristle and skin.

2 We chop very fine, dredging with flour and seasoning while chopping.

3 We put it in the frying-pan with a little hot water and butter.

4 We set it where it will cook slowly.

5 We make small pieces of toast without any crust.

6 We place them on a hot platter and arrange the hash nicely upon them.

Now it is finished.

### BOILED CORNED BEEF.

1 We put it into a bowl of water to rinse it.
2 We plunge it into a pot of boiling water.
3 In ten minutes we put it on back of stove to cook more slowly.
4 We let it simmer till tender.
5 When it is cooked we let it cool in the pot.
Now it is finished.

### WARMED-OVER MEAT.

1 We lay the bone and trimmings in the frying-pan.
2 We cut in a little onion or salt pork.
3 We put it on the stove to brown.
4 We cut the meat thin across the grain.

5  We turn hot water into the pan for the gravy.
6  We strain it into a bowl.
7  We rinse all the specks from the frying-pan.
8  We turn the gravy into the frying-pan and stand it on the stove.
9  We prepare the thickening.
10  We add it to the boiling gravy.
11  We season and taste.  (The flour should taste cooked.)
12  We add the meat to the gravy.
13  We set it where it will heat slowly.
When hot it is finished.

### MEAT ESCALOPED.

1  We wash and pare our potatoes into cold water.
2  We cut them into quarters, and put in saucepan to boil.
3  We cut and trim any fresh meat into a tray.
4  We chop the meat very fine.
5  We dredge in flour and seasoning while chopping.
6  We add butter and hot water till sufficiently moist.
7  We turn it into a vegetable-dish.
8  We mash and season the potatoes.  (As for mashed potatoes.)
9  We place it on the top of the meat smoothly.
10  We spread it over with butter.
11  We cut it across that the crust may not bind.
12  We place it in the oven to brown.
Now it is finished.

*All of these meats should be carried to the class cooked, and some of them chopped.*

## LESSON FIFTH.

### DIAGRAM OF TABLES.

```
┌─────────────────────────────────────────────┐
│            TEACHER'S TABLE.                 │
│                                             │
│   Water, Meat,                              │
│   Flour, Butter,         Necessary Dishes.  │
│   Salt.                                     │
└─────────────────────────────────────────────┘
```

```
┌─────────────────────┐        ┌─────────────────────────┐
│        O            │        │         O               │
│                     │        │                         │
│  O  Saucepan.       │        │   Gridiron.          O  │
│                     │        │   Saucepan.             │
│                     │        │   Table-spoons.         │
│                     │        │                         │
│  O  Bowl, Water,    │        │   Bowl of Water,     O  │
│     Towel.          │        │   Towel.                │
│                     │        │                         │
│  O  Two Table-      │        │   Dredging-boxes of  O  │
│     spoons.         │        │   Salt and Flour.       │
│                     │        │   Teacup and Spoon.     │
│                     │        │                         │
│  O  Spider,         │        │   Dripping-pan and   O  │
│     Dredging-box,   │        │   Rack, Two             │
│     Salt, Flour.    │        │   Table-spoons.         │
│                     │        │                         │
│        O            │        │         O               │
└─────────────────────┘        └─────────────────────────┘
```

```
        ┌──────────────┐
        │    STOVE.    │
        │              │
        │    Kettle.   │
        └──────────────┘
```

# LESSON SIXTH.

# SIXTH COOKING LESSON.

## BILL OF FARE.

### BREAD.

### FRENCH ROLLS.

### FRIED DOUGH.

### RAISED BISCUIT.

### CINNAMON BREAD.

*Utensils Needed.*

- 4 Moulding-boards.
- 2 Rolling-pins.
- 2 Square Loaf-pans.
- 2 Pans for Rolls.
- 2 Pans for Biscuit.
- 1 Kettle.
- 1 Skimmer.
- 2 Towels.

- 1 Dredging-box.
- 2 Cups.
- 1 Quart Measure.
- 1 Sifter.
- 2 Forks.
- 4 Plates.
- 1 Table-spoon.
- 1 Large Platter.

Plates for Bread and Biscuit.

### MATERIAL REQUIRED.

- 6 Quarts of Flour.
- 2 Lbs. of Lard.
- ¼ Lb. of Butter.
- ½ Pint of Milk.

- 1¼ Yeast Cakes, Fleischman's.
- 1½ Table-spoonfuls of Salt.
- 1½ Table-spoonfuls of Sugar.

## LESSON SIXTH.

### EXPENSE OF LESSON.

| | |
|---|---|
| Flour | $0 30 |
| Milk | 02 |
| Butter | 12 |
| Lard | 14 |
| Yeast | 04 |
| Salt and Sugar | 01 |
| | $0 63 |

# Order of Exercise.

### MARCH.

### CHORD—BE SEATED.

### Song—"*Bread Making.*"

### *Lecture.*

### *A few Questions.*

### *Read Bill of Fare.*

Appoint three girls to each receipt.

Teacher have bowl of dough ready to knead into loaves, rolls, biscuits, and fried dough.

Have all the girls see this in mass.

Teacher have ready prepared a loaf, rolls, and biscuits in pans, for the oven, also some dough for frying, to show the girls how these look.

Appoint one or two girls to attend to the baking of these.

Teacher divide dough to be kneaded into four parts, allowing less than one-quarter for frying.

Teacher show girls how to knead, how to cut dough for frying, and how to mould into French rolls and biscuits.

Have lard heating, and give as many girls a chance to fry as possible.

When kneading, moulding and frying are done, have girls take their seats and draw cuts to know who shall mix a new batch.

This being decided, have class direct the mixing.

Let the girl who mixes take home the dough to bake.

Class taste what has been cooked.

### *Dismiss after Song.*

## LETTER ON BREAD.

To-day you are to have a lesson on bread making, and I want you to learn all that the flour contains, and how it affects your health.

But, *first*, we will talk about how to make bread, rolls, and biscuit. All three are to be made out of the same dough, so if you listen closely and learn how to make the batch of bread, you will know what it all starts from.

Here in this bowl is dough all ready for kneading, and here, materials that are put in it. I know you all buy your bread, and it is the easiest way, perhaps; but it takes a great deal more baker's bread to satisfy hunger than home-made bread, and the latter is more nourishing.

So, if there is a large family of children at home, it will be well to know how to make home-made bread.

Then, again, you can make so many nice dishes with bread dough as a basis—crust for a pot-pie, raised doughnuts, and a healthful cake; and in cold weather one can keep the dough several days, and so have hot rolls for breakfast and supper with very little trouble.

You may not always live in the city, where you can buy bread so conveniently.

Then, if you should ever live in other homes, you would need to know how to make good bread, as no one is considered a perfect cook who does not understand bread making, and I want you to give good attention, for I should not be willing to say that my scholars did not know how to make bread. The yeast that bread is raised with is made from a plant.

Some yeast is made of hops, and brewer's yeast of another plant, that ferments in little bubbles, like soap-bubbles. When this yeast is mixed in the flour, it fills the dough with air-bubbles, that lift, or *raise*, as we say, every part of it.

In warm weather yeast works twice as fast as in cold weather, and both too great heat or cold will kill it; and if water is too hot with which you mix your dough, it will kill the yeast, so that water or milk with which you mix your bread must be *lukewarm*. The milk should be scalded and then allowed to cool, as the acid in unscalded milk may sour the bread; the only way to know if it is right heat is to feel with your finger.

All know that you should use sifted flour in cooking, but it makes a great difference whether flour is sifted before or after measuring. This rule on the Receipt Chart is to be sifted after it is measured, so you can put your sieve on the top of the bowl in which it is to be mixed, and salt and flour can be sifted through together.

Then make a hole in the flour, not quite to the bottom of it, or the china is seen, and the yeast would stick to it.

Then mix part of the water and yeast together, and pour into the hole just a little at a time, so you can mix flour and water gradually toward the middle until it has been made into dough; mix well together.

Spread a little flour on the board, and heap a little on one side, enough to knead dough. When none of the dough sticks to your hands you can leave off kneading, but not until then, as rested dough is not near so nice. Rub a little melted lard over top of dough, then cover with clean cloth, and put it near the fire. You cannot tell just how long it must stand to rise, but when it rises to double its size it is ready to be made into loaves and put in pans.

This, before it is ready to bake, must rise again; then the top must be pricked or cut across, so that the crust will not bind, and the loaves be put into a quick oven to bake.

The air is hot at the top of the oven, so you must put your bread on the bottom, for if you should bake your dough hard on the top first it would not rise at all, and we wish to have the yeast swell the starch and send the water that is in the dough in steam out through the holes we pricked in the loaf.

When a broom straw will pass through and come out dry, it is done.

When it is taken from the oven it should be placed on its side, or top crust, so that the steam can get out of the bottom of the loaf, which is not so hard as the top crust.

Now you know how to make the bread, I will repeat some things I have told you before—that the flour is made up of albumen or gluten, which makes our flesh, muscles, and nerves; starch, which makes our fat; and phosphorus, lime, and gelatine, which make our bones grow hard and strong.

Starch is a very white substance, and not very nourishing, although it makes us fat. Gluten, phosphorus, gelatine, and lime, which feed our muscles and nerves and make the bones strong, are dark-colored substances; so it does not follow that because flour is not very white it is not good.

It may have more health-giving substances in it than the white kind.

Graham flour, which has more of these substances in it, is much darker in color.

You now have your lesson upon handling the dough, and after what you have learned here I hope you will practice at home.

---

QUESTIONS.

*Question. How many articles are needed in making bread?*
*Answer.* Six. Flour, salt, water, shortening, yeast, and sugar.
*Q. Must water be hot or cold?*
*A.* Lukewarm.
*Q. When should it be put in?*
*A.* When the flour is quite dry.
*Q. How much salt to a quart of flour?*
*A.* A small teaspoonful.
*Q. How much yeast to a quart of flour?*
*A.* Quarter cake compressed yeast, or quarter cup of liquid yeast.
*Q. Must it be left in a warm or cool place to rise?*
*A.* In a warm place.
*Q. After it is moulded into loaves is it baked at once?*
*A.* No; it is left to get light.
*Q. How do you know when it is ready?*
*A.* When it is double its original size.
*Q. How should the oven be when it is put in?*
*A.* Hot.
*Q. Should it be kept so?*
*A.* No; it should gradually cool off.

## LESSON SIXTH.

*Q.* How do you know when it is done?

*A.* By a broom straw being passed through and coming out perfectly dry.

*Q.* When baked, how is bread cared for?

*A.* Turned upside down, and wrapped in a cloth till cool, to steam crust and make it tender; or rub over the top with butter or lard.

*Q.* What is the last thing you do to your dough before covering it?

*A.* Rub lard over the top of it.

*Q.* What is this for?

*A.* To prevent a hard crust forming.

*Q.* How are French rolls made?

*A.* The dough is rolled about an inch thick, then cut with a biscuit-cutter. Rub a little butter around half the edge, then turn over till almost double. The rolls should be very light before they are baked.

*Q.* How are biscuits made?

*A.* The dough is rolled out, then cut in little pieces of same size, turned into rounds with the fingers, and put side by side in the pan. Cover them with a towel, and set near the fire to rise.

*Q.* What makes fried bread particularly convenient?

*A.* In the morning, before oven is heated or biscuit raised, the simple dough would expand in hot fat, and it could be much more quickly cooked.

# RECEIPTS.

### BREAD.

2 Quarts of flour.
About three-quarters of a quart of water.
½ Table-spoonful of salt, sugar, and lard.
½ Cup of liquid yeast, or ½ cake of compressed yeast.

Sift the flour into the bread-bowl, take out a cupful of it to use in kneading the bread. Then add salt, sugar, lard, yeast, and the water, which must be lukewarm. Mix thoroughly, then dredge board with flour, and turn dough out on it. Knead from twenty to thirty minutes; put back in bowl. Rub melted lard over the top of the dough, cover closely, and set in a warm place to rise.

### FRENCH ROLLS.

Use a part of the bread dough, and follow the recapitulation of the lesson.

### POWDER BISCUIT.

1 Quart flour, 2 heaping table-spoonfuls of shortening, half lard and half butter.
2 Cups of milk.
2 Heaping teaspoonfuls of baking-powder.
Salt-spoonful of salt.

Sift the flour, baking-powder, and salt, three times; then rub the shortening in the flour lightly with the hands; add the milk gradually. When mixed, turn on floured board, roll out lightly, and cut in cakes half an inch thick. Bake in quick oven.

### FRIED DOUGH.

When bread dough is light, roll out about an inch thick, cut in even lengths two inches long and one-half wide. Let these rise. Then drop into boiling fat, constantly turning them. When a light brown on each side, remove with a skimmer to a hot dish.

They are very nice with coffee.

## LESSON SIXTH.

#### CINNAMON BREAD.

Roll out either yeast dough, or baking-powder dough, about half inch thick. Spread it with melted butter, powder it with sugar and a little powdered cinnamon, roll it like jelly-cake, and cut across in slices. If raised, it must stand awhile before going into the oven.

### *Recapitulation of the Lesson.*

#### BREAD.

1  We dissolve the yeast in a little water.
2  We measure the milk, add the warm water and lard to it.
3  We measure the flour, salt, and sugar into the sieve.
4  We sift the flour into the bowl.
5  We make a hole in the flour, not quite to the bottom.
6  We turn the yeast into this well, and some of the milk and water.
7  We mix toward the middle.
8  If more water is needed, turn it where the flour seems dry.
9  We knead with one hand till the bowl is clean.
10  Next we dredge a little flour on the moulding-board.
11  We turn the ball of dough on it.
12  We knead it from twenty to thirty minutes.
13  We place it in the bowl, smooth side up.
14  We hold a little lard in the hand till warm, and then rub it over the dough.
15  We lay a clean towel over it.
16  We cover it with the moulding-board, a pan, or a tin cover.

#### FRENCH ROLLS.

1  We flour the moulding-board.
2  We shape some of the raised dough into a ball.
3  We flour the rolling-pin.
4  We roll the dough from us till about an inch thick.
5  We cut it with a biscuit-cutter.
6  We dip one finger into some butter, and butter one-half of the edge of each piece.

7 We fold the unbuttered half over the buttered, and place in the pan in which they are to be baked.

8 We place them near the fire to rise until double their original size.

9 Then we bake.

### FRIED DOUGH.

1 We flour the moulding-board.
2 We shape some of the raised dough into a ball.
3 We flour the rolling-pin.
4 We roll the dough from us till about an inch thick.
5 We cut in strips about two inches long and half inch wide.
6 We place frying-pan on to heat, in which we put some butter and lard.
7 We drop some of the pieces of dough into the boiling fat.
8 We turn them constantly.
9 When a light brown they are finished.

## LESSON SIXTH.

### DIAGRAM OF TABLES.

```
┌─────────────────────────────────────────────────┐
│              TEACHER'S TABLE.                    │
│                                                  │
│  Two Cups,    Loaf in Tin,        Lard,          │
│  Table-spoon, Rolls in Tin,       Qt. Measure    │
│  Moulding-   Biscuit in Tin,        of Flour,    │
│    board,    Mixing-bowl of Dough, Salt,         │
│  Pint Measure. Large Platter,     Yeast,         │
│               Two Plates.         Sugar.         │
└─────────────────────────────────────────────────┘
```

```
┌──────────────────────┐      ┌──────────────────────┐
│          o           │      │          o           │
│  o                   │      │                    o │
│   Moulding-board,    │      │   Kettle and Skimmer,│
│   Tin for Biscuit,   │      │   Plate,             │
│   Plate of Flour.    │      │   Moulding-board,    │
│                      │      │   Plate of Flour,    │
│                      │      │   Knife,             │
│                      │      │   Rolling-pin.       │
│  o                   │      │                    o │
│                      │      │                      │
│                      │      │                      │
│  o                   │      │                    o │
│   Plate of Flour,    │      │   Moulding-board,    │
│   Moulding-board,    │      │   Tin for a Loaf,    │
│   Rolling-pin,       │      │   Plate of Flour.    │
│   Knife,             │      │                      │
│  o Tin for Rolls.    │      │                    o │
│          o           │      │          o           │
└──────────────────────┘      └──────────────────────┘
```

```
        ┌──────────────────┐
        │  LARD-HEATING    │
        │     STOVE.       │
        │                  │
        │     Kettle.      │
        └──────────────────┘
```

# LESSON SEVENTH.

## VEGETABLE LESSON.

### BILL OF FARE.

MINCED SPINACH.

CREAM CARROTS.

FRIED PARSNIPS.

STEWED OYSTER-PLANT.

SCALLOPED TOMATOES.

*Utensils Needed.*

- 12 Boards and Pans.
- 12 Knives.
- 3 Saucepans and Covers.
- Colander.
- Small Saucepan.
- Large Porcelain Kettle and Cover.
- Pail or Cup to boil Egg.
- Chopping-bowl and Knife.
- Large Pan in which to wash the Spinach.
- 2 Cups.
- 2 Frying-pans.
- 2 Teaspoons.
- 4 Table-spoons.
- 4 Forks.

### MATERIALS REQUIRED—EXPENSE.

| | | |
|---|---|---|
| 2 | Small Carrots | $0 03 |
| 1 | Bunch Oyster-plant | 12 |
| 2 | Parsnips | 04 |
| 1 | Pint of Milk | 04 |
| ¼ | Lb. of Butter | 12 |
| | Baking soda | 01 |
| | Lard, Flour | 02 |
| | Salt, Pepper | 01 |
| 1 | Quart of Spinach | 15 |
| 1 | Egg | 03 |
| | | $0 57 |

N. B.—Have 1 carrot, 1 parsnip, and part of oyster-plant cooked.

# Order of Exercise.

### MARCH.

CHORD—BE SEATED.

SONG—"*Vegetable.*"

*Lecture.*

*A few Questions.*

*Read Bill of Fare.*

Appoint three girls to each receipt.
Have vegetables washed and roots scraped.
Teacher call special attention to the washing of spinach, and explain the way.
Have all put on to boil as quickly as possible.
Egg should be put on in cold water and remain on stove for half an hour, then dropped in cold water till ready to use.
While carrots are boiling, have dressing prepared.
Before carrots, parsnips, and oyster-plants are boiled, have them cut according to receipts.
When parsnips are tender, drain and put them to cool before frying.
While vegetables are boiling, have girls copy receipts.
When all is cooked, have girls taste and express opinions.
Teacher ask a few questions.

*Sing, if time; then dismiss class.*

## LETTER ON VEGETABLES.

To-day our lesson is on vegetables. Every food that has grown in the ground is called a vegetable ; and to explain it to you in the simplest way, I will divide them into classes.

Here are *Seeds*, such as wheat, oats, corn, rice, etc.

*Roots*, such as carrots, oyster-plants, beets, potatoes, parsnips.

*Leaves*, as spinach, lettuce, all kinds of greens.

*Stems*, like celery, rhubarb, asparagus.

The seeds all contain more starch than anything else, and the skin of all these seeds cracks in the boiling water, the inside swells and becomes gummy.

Therefore, long boiling is essential for all starched foods.

The roots are mostly vegetables that will last all winter if properly taken care of.

Toward spring you must watch them and pick off the sprouts, lest they become rank.

Soak them to plump them, and cook them with greater care.

The roots are particularly nice when they first come, if quite ripe. When young and tender they require less time to cook.

The *Leaves* should be thoroughly washed and put into salted water just beginning to boil—one table-spoonful of salt to every two quarts of water. The water should be drawn fresh, and the vegetables put in its first boiling, or they will not look a good color.

A bit of soda, size of a pea, is necessary to counteract an unhealthy oil in spinach as well as in all beans.

Nearly all vegetables are dressed with salt and butter, sometimes a little sugar and pepper sprinkled in at the last.

Spinach and cabbage are apt to be sandy unless carefully looked over and washed.

The first washing should be done in warm, not cold water, in which it should be shaken up and down, but not allowed to lie.

Asparagus and celery are both cooked as a vegetable, and seasoned with butter and salt; but rhubarb, which is more for a sauce, has only sugar cooked in it.

In a city like New York all varieties are in the market nearly all the months of the year; but not until they are growing near where we live can we expect to find them cheap.

During the summer, if you can get them fresh and cook them nicely, you will not need to buy near as much meat, and can make many nice dishes, mostly all vegetables.

---

*Question. How are vegetables divided?*

*Answer.* Into four classes : *Roots*, such as carrots. *Seeds*, as oats, rice, etc. *Leaves*, as spinach, lettuce, etc. *Stems*, as asparagus, celery, etc.

*Q. How should the* ROOTS *be prepared for cooking?*

*A.* Washed and scraped.

*Q. How should the* LEAVES *be prepared?*

*A.* Thoroughly washed and carefully looked over.

*Q. In salting the water for vegetables, what are the proportions?*

*A.* One table-spoonful of salt to two quarts of water.

*Q. In boiling spinach and beans, what should be put into the water?*

*A.* A bit of soda size of a pea.

*Q. What is this for?*

*A.* To make the greens a good color, and to correct the effects of an unhealthy oil which is in spinach.

*Q. How should spinach be washed?*

*A.* First in warm (not hot) water, dipped in and out, but not allowed to lie.

*Q. How is rhubarb used?*

*A.* As a sauce, and is seasoned with sugar.

# RECEIPTS.

### MINCED SPINACH.

Wash carefully, put into salted boiling water with soda size of a pea.

When tender, drain in colander and chop fine.

For each quart of chopped spinach put two table-spoonfuls of butter and one of flour in frying-pan, and when this has cooked smooth, and before it has browned, add the spinach, stir in a cup of milk, and when thoroughly heated remove.

Arrange spinach in a mound on a hot dish, with slices of cold boiled egg on top.

### CREAM CARROTS.

Wash and scrape, cut into dice, put into boiling water slightly salted, and boil until tender; drain, and serve with a dressing made of one table-spoonful of butter, one of flour, rubbed together and stirred into a cup of *hot milk*. Let it come to a boil, and pour over the carrots.

### FRIED PARSNIPS.

Scrape and boil the parsnips in salted boiling water. When tender, drain, slice lengthwise, dredge with flour, and fry in hot lard, or half lard and half butter. Season and serve.

### ESCALOPED TOMATOES.

One pint of tomatoes, half cup of bread-crumbs, a little butter and flour. Put a layer of bread-crumbs in the bottom of a baking-dish, season them with salt, pepper, and butter. Then a layer of tomatoes dredged with flour and seasoned. Continue till the dish is full, having the crumbs on the top.

*Recapitulation of the Lesson.*

### MINCED SPINACH.

1 We place two pails, one with very hot and one with cold water, side by side.

2 We pick up the spinach in small bunches.
3 We dash them, leaves downward, into the hot water, then throw them into the cold.
4 We pick them out of the cold water, cutting off the roots and poor leaves.
5 We put them into a saucepan with salted boiling water.
6 We put an egg to boil to dress it.
7 We put soda the size of a pea into the boiling spinach when nearly cooked.
8 Boil until tender, then drain in a colander.
9 We rub butter and flour together.
10 We chop and measure the spinach.
11 We put butter and flour into a frying-pan, and cook smooth.
12 We add the chopped spinach.
13 We measure and add the milk.
14 We shell and slice the boiled egg on a plate.
15 Arrange the spinach in a mound on a hot dish.
16 We garnish with sliced egg.
Now it is finished.

### CREAM CARROTS.

1 We scrape and cut the carrots in slices.
2 We put them to boil in salted water.
3 We stir the butter and flour together for thickening.
4 We drain off the water when tender, measure and add the milk.
5 We stir in the thickening.
6 When the flour tastes cooked it is finished.

### FRIED PARSNIPS.

1 We wash and scrape the parsnips.
2 We put them to boil in salted hot water.
3 When tender, we drain and slice lengthwise.
4 We dredge them with flour.
5 We have our saucepan hot, and put in butter and lard sufficient to fry them.
6 We lay in the slices, sprinkle on salt, and brown them.
7 We pile them nicely on a hot dish.
Now they are finished.

*Stewed oyster-plant, cooked just like the cream carrots.*

## ESCALOPED TOMATOES.

1 We grate the bread.
2 We have a layer of crumbs in the bottom of a baking-dish.
3 We put bits of butter upon it.
4 We shake in pepper and salt.
5 We lay in a layer of tomatoes (sliced).
6 We shake on a little flour, bits of butter, salt, and a very little sugar.
7 Then we put on more bread and more tomatoes in the same way until the dish is full.
8 We have the crumbs for the last layer.
9 We put into oven and brown.
Now it is finished.

## LESSON EIGHTH.

### DIAGRAM OF TABLES.

```
┌─────────────────────────────────────────────┐
│              TEACHER'S TABLE.               │
│                                             │
│   Soda.        Cooked Carrot.   Parsnip, etc.│
└─────────────────────────────────────────────┘
```

Frying-pan,
Pan Hot Water,
Pan Cold Water,
Chopping-tray and Knife.
Hot Dish.

Small Saucepan,
Colander,
Butter,
Spinach,
Flour,
Milk.

Hot Dish,
Saucepan,
Butter, Flour,
Table-spoon,
Cup with Plate.

Frying-pan,
Dredging-box, Flour,
Lard and Butter,
Hot Platter.

Baking-dish,
Can Tomatoes,
Stale Bread, Grater,
Salt, Pepper, Butter,
Dredging-box, Flour.

# LESSON EIGHTH.

# EIGHTH COOKING LESSON.

## BILL OF FARE.

#### BROILED FISH.

#### BOILED FISH.

#### FRIED FISH.

#### BAKED FISH.

#### FLAKED FISH.

#### MATERIAL REQUIRED—EXPENSE.

| | | |
|---|---|---|
| 3 | Pan-fish | $0 10 |
| 1 | Fish to boil | 20 |
| 1 | Fish to broil | 10 |
| 1 | Fish to bake | 25 |
| ½ | Lb. of Salt Pork | 09 |
| 1 | Bunch of Parsley | 03 |
| 1 | Egg | 03 |
| ¼ | Lb. of Butter | 12 |
| ½ | Pint of Vinegar | 02 |
| | Flour, Salt | 02 |
| | Pepper | 01 |
| | Water | 00 |
| ½ | Lb. of Indian Meal | 02 |
| | | $0 99 |

## LESSON EIGHTH.

*Articles Needed.*

1 Dripping-pan.
1 Boiling-kettle.
1 Skimmer.
3 Bowls.
4 Thick pieces of Paper to put Fish on.
Cloth to wrap boiled Fish in.
Needle and Cotton.
3 Towels.
Small Saucepan or Tin Cup to boil Egg in.
1 Teacup.
4 Table-spoons.
Dredging-boxes of Salt and Flour.
Cake-turner.

# Order of Exercise.

MARCH.

CHORD—BE SEATED.

SONG—"*Marketing.*"

*Lecture.*

*A few Questions.*

*Read Bill of Fare.*

Appoint three girls to each receipt.
One of each three bring paper to teacher's table for fish.
Wash and prepare fish for cooking.
Have baked fish started cooking first.
Let entire class see how this is dressed and arranged for the oven.
Then the fish to be boiled should be put in the kettle. Have girls see how this is served in the cloth to fit its shape, and without any unnecessary lapping of the cloth.
The frying-pan should then be put on to heat, in which first brown some pieces of pork, then fry the smelts.
Let the three girls fry, each one fish in turn.
When the fire is best, broil mackerel.
When all is cooked, have the girls garnish the different dishes with parsley.
While fish is hot have it *tasted* and *tested*.
After meal have a review of questions.

*Dismiss class.*

## LETTER ON FISH.

To-day our lesson is to be upon fish. It is a very healthful and digestible food. Though not nearly so nutritious as meat, it is considered by many physicians a good brain food, especially if it is broiled

The culture of fish is very remarkable. In the last ten years a rapid advance has been made in this, and they are raised in large quantities as poultry is, and really add greatly to the food supply of the people. In 1856 the Massachusetts government took so much interest in the raising of fish as to bring the subject before the Legislature, and ever since then it has been a growing interest.

Germany is far ahead of other countries in raising fish.

France has done something about it, and so has England; but at a recent meeting to organize a national fish association, Lord Exeter plainly told the English fish-culturists that they were not up to the times. I simply mention this to show you how important a subject this is, and that we are not losing time in learning to cook food well that is in such general use. There is such a large variety of fish, it would take too much time and space to fully describe all, so I will only tell of the more common kinds which you will be apt to find in market.

The cod, white-fish, striped bass, smelts, black-fish, flounders, and halibut, will be found all the year round.

The shad, in Eastern and Middle States, will be found from March till the end of April, and in the Southern States from November to February.

The blue-fish is through June, July, and August; the mackerel through spring and summer.

The Spanish mackerel from June to October. The pan-fish, as they are called, are small fish, and mostly fried.

The halibut, salmon, sword-fish, and sturgeon, are all very large fish, and are sold in pieces.

The haddock differs slightly from the cod. The cod has a light stripe running down the side, and haddock a dark one.

The haddock is a firmer and smaller flaked fish. The white-fish have far less oil distributed through their bodies, and therefore are not so rich as the darker colored fish. They need richer sauces and dressings.

Fish should be selected with great care. The skin and scales should be bright, the eyes full and clear, and the fins stiff.

Although they should be cleaned at the market, one should not trust entirely to such cleaning, but pass the edge of the knife over the fish, to remove any remaining scales. Wash it inside and out with a wet cloth, and dry carefully with a towel.

In this lesson you will learn but the four ordinary ways of cooking fish.

After you know these you will be able to use other receipts with more judgment, as nearly all fish of the same family require the same kind of cooking. If you know how to boil, broil, fry, and bake nicely we will perhaps take up the shell-fish, and more expensive fish later.

Your teachers will show you exactly how to follow the receipts printed on the charts, and I shall hope to hear of great success in your fish lesson.

### QUESTIONS ON FISH.

*Question.* Is fish good food?
*Answer.* Yes; but not so nutritious as meat.
*Q.* What do physicians say of it?
*A.* It is a good brain food.
*Q.* Is the culture of fish progressing?
*A.* Yes; and is adding greatly to our food supply.
*Q.* What nation is in the advance?
*A.* Germany.
*Q.* Name some of the fish in market all the year round.
*A.* Cod, striped bass, flounders, black-fish, white-fish, smelts, and halibut.
*Q.* What term is given to the small fish?
*A.* Pan-fish, and they are mostly fried.
*Q.* How are the large fish sold, such as salmon, halibut, and sturgeon?
*A.* In pieces, or steaks.

## LESSON EIGHTH.

*Q. How does the haddock differ from the cod?*
*A.* The cod has a light stripe running down the side, and the haddock a dark one.
*Q. In what other respects do they differ?*
*A.* The haddock is a firmer and smaller-flaked fish.
*Q. Which is the richer, dark fish, or light?*
*A.* The dark fish, as they have more oil in their bodies.
*Q. In buying, what should you notice?*
*A.* Whether the eyes are full and clear, the scales bright, and the fins stiff.
*Q. Is it necessary to clean them after the fish man?*
*A.* Yes; they should be washed inside and out, and thoroughly dried.
*Q. What are the four ordinary ways of cooking fish?*
*A.* Broiling, boiling, frying, and baking.

# RECEIPTS.

### TO BROIL FISH.

Heat gridiron, and lard it to prevent fish sticking. Put flesh side down. Mix some butter, pepper, and salt together on a platter. Lay fish in this, and put a little butter on fish.

### TO BOIL FISH.

Wash fish, and rub carefully with a little vinegar. Boil in salted boiling water, in which put one table-spoonful of vinegar. Allow ten minutes to a pound. Try with a sharp-pointed needle; if it runs through easily it is done.

Open cloth on a sieve or strainer.

### TO FRY FISH.

Cleanse thoroughly, dry on a folded cloth, roll in Indian meal, and fry with pieces of pork and lard. Have clear, hot fire.

### TO BAKE FISH.

Wash and dry on a towel. Gash fish straight across, half inch deep and two inches long, and one inch apart, and lay in strips of pork. Place in pan, and cover the bottom with water half inch deep; add one dessert-spoonful of butter and one salt-spoonful of salt. Dredge fish with flour, and baste often. Keep up your supply of gravy as it boils away. Try with a knitting-needle, and take up with a cake-turner.

### DRAWN BUTTER OR SAUCE FOR FISH.

Half cup of butter, half table-spoonful of flour, one salt-spoonful of salt, one hard-boiled egg, half cup of boiling water or milk. Cut up egg in sauce-tureen, mix butter, flour, and salt to a cream, moisten with hot water; add this to the half cup of boiling water in saucepan over fire. Let it cook till it thickens smoothly. When ready to serve, pour it over the chopped egg, stir together, and add small bits of parsley.

*Recapitulation of Fish Lesson.*

### TO BROIL FISH.

1 We scrape and wipe the fish carefully.

2 We heat the platter.

3 We put butter, salt, and pepper on the platter, and leave it in a warm place.

4 We warm the gridiron, and put the fish upon it.

5 We lay the gridiron over the coals, the flesh side of the fish down.

6 We stand by until it is a nice brown.

7 We then turn the skin side down.

8 When cooked, we lay it on the platter, and baste it with the salt, pepper, and butter.

9 We cover with a hot platter until served. We lay it on the platter skin side down.

Now it is finished.

### TO BOIL FISH.

1 We wash the fish and rub it over with a little vinegar.

2 We sew it into a piece of cloth, fitting the shape as nearly as possible.

3 We cover it with salted boiling water, in which put one small teaspoonful of vinegar.

4 We let it boil ten minutes to every pound.

5 We try it with a knitting-needle; if it runs through easily it is done.

6 We raise it from the pot by the cloth, and lay it on an inverted sieve.

7 We prepare the platter to receive the fish by folding a napkin, the size of the fish, upon it.

8 We rip open the cloth, and slip it on the platter prepared for it. Now it is finished.

## LESSON EIGHTH.

### TO BAKE FISH.

1 We wash and dry the fish inside and out with a towel.

2 We gash it across, one-half inch deep, two inches long, and one inch apart.

3 We make a dressing of salt pork, bread-crumbs, a little salt and pepper, chopped together.

4 We lay the dressing inside the fish, and sew it up.

5 We put narrow strips of salt pork into the gashes on the fish.

6 We lay it on a strip of tin the size of the fish.

7 Then we lay tin and all into the baking-pan.

8 We set it into the oven.

9 We dredge fish with flour.

10 We turn in water half inch deep, and dessert-spoonful of butter, and salt-spoonful of salt.

11 We baste often.

12 If water boils away we add more.

13 Try with knitting-needle to see if done.

14 When done, we lift fish and tin out of the baking-pan.

15 We slip fish on hot platter, and serve.

Now it is finished.

### TO FRY FISH.

1 We wash and dry the fish.

2 We put some pieces of salt pork to fry.

3 We salt the fish and dip them in Indian meal.

4 If not sufficient fat to fry the fish, we add a little lard.

5 We lay in the fish, and stand by until brown.

6 We turn them on the other side, and when a light brown they are done.

7 We place them on a hot platter.

Now they are finished.

## LESSON EIGHTH.

### DIAGRAM OF TABLES.

```
TEACHER'S TABLE.

Water,      Egg,
Flour,      Fish,        Necessary Dishes.
Butter.     Pork.
```

Bowl,
Boiling-kettle,
Paper for Fish,
Half cup of Vinegar,
Table-spoon,
Cup,
Tin Pail.

Towel,
Bowl of Water,
Plate of Parsley.

Frying-pan,
Paper for Fish,
Plate of Indian Meal.

Dripping-pan,
Knife,
Dredging box of Flour and Salt.

Plate for Parsley,
Bowl of Water,
Towel.

Broiler,
Paper for Fish.

```
STOVE.

Kettle.
```

# LESSON NINTH.

# NINTH COOKING LESSON.

## BILL OF FARE.

TOMATO SOUP.

BEAN SOUP.

POTATO SOUP.

PEA SOUP.

*Utensils Required.*

| | |
|---|---|
| 12 Boards. | Small Baking-pan for Toast Crumbs. |
| 4 Saucepans. | Pint Measure. |
| 3 Colanders. | Strainer. |
| Sieve. | 3 Forks. |
| Soup-ladle. | Small Saucepan. |
| ½ Dozen Table-spoons | Bowl. |
| 3 Tin Pans to drop Vegetables in when scraped. | Frying-pan. |

MATERIAL USED—EXPENSE.

| | |
|---|---|
| Can of Tomatoes | $0 12 |
| ½ Pint of White Beans | 08 |
| ½ Pint of Split Peas | 05 |
| 1 Pint of Milk | 04 |
| 3 Potatoes | 01 |
| 2 Onions | 02 |
| Celery (a stalk) | 03 |
| ¼ Lb. of Butter | 12 |
| A few Slices of Bread | 01 |
| Flour | 01 |
| Salt, Pepper | 01 |
| ½ Lb. of Salt Pork | 08 |
| | $0 58 |

# Order of Exercise.

MARCH.

CHORD—BE SEATED.

SONG—"*Vegetable.*"

*Lecture.*

*A few Questions.*

*Read Bill of Fare.*

Appoint three girls to each receipt.
Make half of each receipt.
Teacher have *pea* and *bean* soup partially cooked.
Have potatoes boiled for potato soup, milk and seasoning boiling; but do not put together until the last thing, as potato soup should *not* stand, even if kept hot.
Have girls season pea and bean soup.
Have tomatoes put on to boil. While these are cooking have girls prepare thickening.
The girls that are not busy cooking copy receipts.
When all the soups are cooked, have class taste.

*Review Questions.*

# LETTER ON SOUP.

Our lesson is to be soups.

French, Germans, and Americans, rich and poor, have some kind of soup every day.

Some people depend upon it for an entire meal, and some only for a first course of a dinner.

Soups are made with stock. A *purée*, which is merely thick soup, is generally made of vegetables, and clear soups must be made of uncooked meat.

Stock is only the water in which meat has been boiled. It should be made the day before it is to be used, and the cake of fat which will rise on the top taken off before it is heated over.

If you leave the fat on until it is heated, the stock will keep better.

Never cook vegetables in with the stock that is not to be used immediately, as the juices from the vegetables will cause it to ferment.

Excellent stock can be made from the scraps and bones, cooked or uncooked, that are left from roasts and beefsteaks, and this is the only way of gaining the last bit of nourishment in them.

Whether the meat is cooked or uncooked, it should all be cut in small pieces, and the bones broken.

There is a great deal of gelatine in meat and bones (the same that we buy to make jelly), that thickens and strengthens the soup stock.

But clear gelatine is not nourishing, and boiling the stock *hard* takes away its nourishing properties, and causes the albumen to harden and rise with the scum.

It is necessary to have uncooked meat for clear soups, and all soup should be started in cold water, and uncooked meat and bones washed thoroughly, but quickly, in hot water before being put on the fire in cold water.

When the juices have been extracted from the meat, the liquor should be strained into a stone jar.

Allow one pound of meat and bone to one quart of water in making stock, and be particular to keep closely covered, but skim carefully the first part of the cooking. A cup of cold water poured in will make the scum rise freely. It takes so long to make the stock from meat, as it requires such slow cooking, that we cannot make it in the class; but to-day we will make some *purée*, which, you will remember, I said was mostly made from vegetables, and some of thickened milk, flavored with vegetables. No soup should be thicker than thick cream, and a fat soup is never nice. I have now given you the principal points in making soup, but only experience can teach you to season properly and make a variety.

But I trust with this information you will practice at home, for nothing adds more to a good dinner than an appetizing soup.

---

QUESTIONS ON SOUPS.

*Question. What part of a dinner is the soup?*
*Answer.* The first course.
*Q. What is a purée?*
*A.* A thick soup generally made of vegetables.
*Q. What is stock?*
*A.* It is the liquor in which meat has been boiled.
*Q. If you want to keep the stock any length of time, should you cook vegetables in with it?*
*A.* No. The juices from them will cause it to ferment.
*Q. The fat that rises on the top when the stock is cold—should it be removed?*
*A.* Not until it is to be heated, as it keeps the stock better.
*Q. What is stock made of?*
*A.* Scraps of meat and bones, of cooked or uncooked meat, that are left of roasts and beefsteaks.
*Q. How should the meat be prepared?*
*A.* It should all be cut in small pieces, and the bones broken.
*Q. How should stock be boiled?*
*A.* Slowly.
*Q. What kind of meat is necessary for clear soups?*
*A.* Uncooked meat.
*Q. What should first be done with the meat?*
*A.* It should be thoroughly but quickly washed in hot water.

*Q. Should it be put on to cook in hot or cold water?*
*A.* In cold water.
*Q. What should be done when all the juices are extracted from the meat?*
*A.* The liquor should be strained into a stone jar.
*Q. What are the proportions of meat and water?*
*A.* One pound of meat and bone to one quart of water.
*Q. What is to be done the first part of the cooking?*
*A.* The scum taken off.
*Q. What will make it rise to the top?*
*A.* A cup of cold water.

# RECEIPTS.

### TOMATO SOUP.

One quart can of tomatoes, two heaping table-spoonfuls of flour, one of butter, one teaspoonful of salt, one pint of hot water, one teaspoonful of sugar. Rub flour and butter together with a tablespoonful of tomato, stir into the boiling mixture, add seasoning; boil all together fifteen minutes. Rub through a sieve, and serve with toast crumbs.

### BEAN SOUP.

Quarter pint of beans, a small piece of salt pork, one and a half pints of cold water, quarter of small onion cut fine, quarter tablespoonful of salt. Cover closely, and boil four or five hours. Rub through a colander.

### POTATO SOUP.

One quart of milk, half dozen large potatoes, one stalk of celery, one tablespoonful of butter, one onion. Pare and boil potatoes thirty minutes. Put milk on to boil with onion and celery, then add the potatoes mashed fine, butter (into which a table-spoonful of flour has been well stirred) and salt. Rub through a colander, and serve immediately. Must not stand. Use a wooden spoon.

### PEA SOUP.

Quarter pint of peas, one pint of cold water, one small strip of salt pork, small salt-spoonful of salt, a little celery seed; fry a small piece of onion till brown Cover closely, and boil all together four or five hours. Rub through a colander.

### STOCK.

Take three pounds of neck piece of beef, three quarts of unsalted water. Let it simmer for six hours; salt, and strain into a stone jar.

## LESSON NINTH.

*Recapitulation of the Lesson.*

### TOMATO SOUP.

1 We open the can of tomatoes.
2 We take out a cupful from the can.
3 We put the rest of the tomato into a porcelain-lined saucepan.
4 We rinse the can with a pint of boiling water, add it to the tomato, and put on to cook.
5 We rub butter and flour together, and stir to it gradually the cup of cold tomato.
6 We add the cold tomato to the mixture when it boils.
7 We cook fifteen minutes.
8 We rub through a sieve and serve.

### BEAN SOUP.

1 We measure and wash the beans.
2 We measure the *cold* water and add to the beans.
3 We scrape and clean one piece of salt pork and put in with beans.
4 We cut our onions, and add to the soup, and cover closely.
5 We boil four or five hours, being careful not to burn.
6 We wet half a teaspoonful of flour smooth, and add to the soup.
7 We rub through a sieve and serve.
Now it is finished.

### POTATO SOUP.

1 We pare the potatoes, and put on to boil.
2 We measure and rub the butter and flour together.
3 We cut the celery and onion into the milk, and put on to heat.
4 When potatoes are cooked, mash them fine.
5 Add the butter and flour to the milk.
6 Then add the mashed potato.
7 When thickened, rub all through a sieve.
8 Serve immediately.

### PEA SOUP.

1 We measure and wash our peas.
2 We measure our cold water, and add to them, and put on to heat.

3 We scrape and cut our strips of salt pork, and fry with a part of an onion
4 We put the onion and pork into the soup.
5 We add a salt-spoonful of celery seed and salt.
6 We cover closely, and boil together four or five hours.
7 When cooked soft we rub through a colander.
Now it is finished.

## LESSON NINTH.

139

### DIAGRAM OF TABLES.

```
┌─────────────────────────────────────────┐
│           TEACHER'S TABLE.              │
│                                         │
│  Pitcher of Cold        Spoons,         │
│      Water,             Forks,          │
│   Milk,       Butter,   Vegetables,     │
│   Flour,      Pork.     Necessary       │
│   Salt,                    Dishes.      │
│   Pepper.                               │
└─────────────────────────────────────────┘
```

```
┌──────────────────┐      ┌──────────────────┐
│       |○         │      │       |○         │
│ ○  Potatoes,     │      │   Saucepan,   ─  │
│ ─  Sieve,        │      │   Pint Measure, ○│
│    Two Saucepans,│      │   Teaspoon,      │
│    Table-spoon,  │      │   Frying-pan,    │
│    Onion.        │      │   Colander.      │
│                  │      │                  │
│ ○                │      │               ─  │
│ ─                │      │               ○  │
│                  │      │                  │
│                  │      │                  │
│ ○                │      │               ─  │
│ ─                │      │               ○  │
│                  │      │                  │
│    Saucepan,     │      │   Pint Measure,  │
│    Pint Measure. │      │   Saucepan and Cover, │
│    Bowl,         │      │   Colander,      │
│ ○  Table-spoon,  │      │   Table-spoon.  ─│
│ ─  Teaspoon.     │      │                  ○│
│                  │      │                  │
│       ○|         │      │       ○|         │
└──────────────────┘      └──────────────────┘
```

```
        ┌──────────────┐
        │    STOVE.    │
        │              │
        │    Kettle.   │
        └──────────────┘
```

# LESSON TENTH.

# TENTH COOKING LESSON.

## BILL OF FARE.

### BREAD PUDDING.

### RICE PUDDING.

### BAKED CUSTARD.

### BOILED CUSTARD.

### LEMON PUDDING.

#### MATERIAL REQUIRED—EXPENSE.

| | |
|---|---|
| 4 Eggs | $0 12 |
| 2 Quarts of Milk | 16 |
| ½ Lb. of Sugar | 05 |
| 2 Table-spoonfuls of Corn-starch | 02 |
| Vanilla Extract | 05 |
| Nutmeg and a few Raisins | 05 |
| | $0 45 |

#### MATERIAL FOR LEMON PUDDING—EXPENSE.

| | |
|---|---|
| 1 Lemon | $0 02 |
| 1 Egg | 03 |
| 1½ Table-spoonfuls of Corn-starch | 01 |
| 5 Table-spoonfuls of Sugar | 01 |
| | $0 07 |

## LESSON TENTH.

*Utensils Needed.*

2 Farina-kettles, or Saucepans, or Pail.
Dripping-pan.
Baking-dish.
Grater (coarse).
Frying-pan.
Skimmer.
Nutmeg-grater.
2 Small Platters.

2 Pint Measures.
½ Doz. Custard-cups.
3 Bowls.
4 Forks.
3 Teaspoons.
4 Table-spoons.
Fancy Glass Dish for boiled Custard.
Dish for Blanc-mange.

# Order of Exercise.

MARCH.

CHORD—BE SEATED.

Song—"*Beating Eggs.*"

*Lecture.*

*A few Questions.*

*Read Bill of Fare.*

Appoint three girls to each receipt.

All girls who break the eggs should separate the yolks from the whites, for practice.

For the boiled custard the yolks and the whites must be beaten separately.

For baked custard, teacher see that the eggs are not beaten too much, and that the nutmeg is put in with the sugar and yolks.

For the boiled custard the milk must come to a boil before the egg, sugar, and corn-starch are stirred in, then stirred constantly.

The baked custard should cook slowly, also the bread pudding.

When the cooking is completed, teacher ask questions. Have a song to close. Song—"*Silly Old Hen.*"

Divide the custards and puddings among the girls.

## LETTER ON DESSERTS.

This is the last lesson which you will receive in this first course of plain cooking, and as, lesson after lesson, you have been learning about the different ingredients you are to use in this, there is little for me to say excepting to help your judgment in the selection of desserts.

When you have a hearty, salt-meat dinner, use a cold, light, delicate pudding, like a boiled custard.

When you have a fish dinner, which does not give the nourishment that meat does, a boiled, hearty pudding.

A lemon corn-starch pudding can be used when you are short of milk, and a broken cold pudding can be made fresh again by arranging it in a clean dish and covering it with a *méringue*.

I have wanted you to enjoy these lessons, so have added these pretty desserts for a treat, and also that, in the variety of dishes all through the course, you may be able to arrange " Bills of Fare" for different meals, if we can have the privilege of lessons next year for the girls who have been learning this year.

I hope through the summer you will review receipts and lessons, and recall all you can of the letters, that you may go on still further another year.

For what should a woman know better than how to conduct and care for a home?

---

### QUESTIONS.

*Question. When you have a hearty dinner, what kind of a pudding or pie should you have?*

*Answer.* A delicate, light pudding.

*Q. When you have a fish or cold meat dinner?*

*A.* A hearty, substantial pudding.

*Q. Which one of the receipts can you use when you have not much milk?*

*A.* A lemon corn-starch pudding.
*Q. Which, when eggs are expensive or scarce?*
*A.* A corn-starch, blanc-mange, or rice pudding.
*Q. How can you warm over some cold puddings?*
*A.* Arrange in a clean dish and put on a *méringue*.

# RECEIPTS.

### BREAD PUDDING.

One pint of milk, half pint of bread-crumbs, one egg, two scant table-spoonfuls of sugar, a few raisins. Soak the bread in the milk, beat the yolk, to which add the sugar, stir into the bread and milk, add the raisins, and bake. Make a *méringue*, for top, of the white of egg well beaten, and one and a half table-spoonfuls of sugar. Brown in the oven.

### RICE PUDDING.

Half cup of rice, one quart of milk, a little salt, two table-spoonfuls of sugar, one teaspoonful of vanilla. Put all in baking-dish, and bake very slowly three or four hours. It should be creamy when done. (Add nutmeg, if you like.)

### BAKED CUSTARD.

One pint of milk, two eggs, one and a half table-spoonfuls of sugar, half teaspoonful of extract, or half of grated nutmeg. Beat eggs (only a little), add sugar and nutmeg while beating, then the milk. Pour into cups, and place in oven in a dripping-pan, with water in the pan.

### BOILED CUSTARD.

One pint of milk, half teaspoonful of flavoring, two eggs, one and a half table-spoonfuls of sugar, one teaspoonful of corn-starch. Heat the milk, then add corn-starch (wet first in a little cold milk), beaten yelks of eggs, and sugar. Cook till of right thickness. Beat the whites to a froth, and cook floating on boiling water for a few minutes. Remove with a skimmer on to an inverted sieve. When custard is cool, place them on top.

### LEMON PUDDING.

One lemon, one egg, one pint of boiling water, three table-spoonfuls of sugar, one and a half table-spoonfuls of corn-starch. Dissolve the corn-starch in a little cold water, put it into the boiling water, also the grated rind of a lemon. Beat the yolk, add the sugar and lemon-juice, and stir into the boiling mixture. When thick, pour into pudding-dish. Make a *méringue* of the white of egg and two table-spoonfuls of granulated sugar, spread over pudding, and brown in the oven.

### CORN-STARCH BLANC-MANGE.

Two table-spoonfuls of corn-starch, one pint of milk, one tea-spoonful of extract vanilla, a little salt. Wet the corn-starch with a little of the milk, and put the remainder on to boil. When it reaches boiling-point, add corn-starch, sugar, and salt. Stir until cooked to taste. Add flavoring, and set away to cool. When cold, serve.

*Recapitulation of the Lesson.*

#### BREAD PUDDING.

1 We grate the bread into the pudding-dish.
2 We measure and turn in the milk.
3 We break the egg, yolk and white separately.
4 We add the sugar to the yolks.
5 We put the raisins in the milk and bread.
6 We grate half teaspoonful of nutmeg into the yelk and sugar, and beat well together.
7 We add the yolk to the bread and milk, and put in oven to bake.
8 We beat the white of egg stiff, and add one table-spoonful of granulated sugar.
9 We try the pudding with the handle of a spoon; if milky, it is not cooked.
10 When done, we spread the white of egg and sugar over the top.
11 When browned a little in a cool oven, it is done.
Now it is finished.

#### RICE PUDDING.

1 We measure, wash, and pick over the rice.
2 We measure the milk.
3 We put them in a dish.
4 We measure and add the flavoring and salt.
5 We add the sugar, and put it in a slow oven to bake three or four hours.

## LESSON TENTH.

### BAKED CUSTARD.

1 We break the eggs into a bowl.
2 We add the sugar and nutmeg.
3 We beat all together.
4 We measure and add the milk, and turn into the cups or dish to bake.
5 We put into a dripping-pan in the oven with water in the pan.
6 We try with a thin knife-blade, or handle of a teaspoon ; if firm, it is finished.

### BOILED CUSTARD.

1 We put a pint of milk into a tin pail.
2 We put this pail into a kettle of boiling water.
3 We measure a table-spoonful of corn-starch into a cup, and wet it with a little of the pint of milk (cold).
4 We break two eggs, whites and yolks separately.
5 We beat the sugar with the yolks.
6 We add the milk and corn-starch to the yolks.
7 When the milk is at boiling-point we add the eggs, sugar, and corn-starch.
8 We stand by and stir till it thickens and tastes cooked.
9 We stand it in a cool place.
10 We put a pan of boiling water on the stove.
11 We beat the whites very stiff and drop in heaps on the boiling water.
12 We add the flavoring to the custard, and turn it into a dish.
13 We drain the whites out with a skimmer on to an inverted sieve.
14 We slip them carefully on the custard.
Now it is finished.

### LEMON PUDDING.

1 Grate the yellow from the rind of the lemon, and squeeze the juice.
2 We put a pint of boiling water in a saucepan over the fire.
3 We measure and wet the corn-starch smooth with a little cold water.
4 We add it to the boiling water in the saucepan, and stir until it thickens.

    5 We add the rind (grated) and juice of the lemon.
    6 We beat the eggs, white and yolk separately.
    7 We stir the beaten yolk into the corn-starch.
    8 We measure and add the sugar.
    9 When cooked, we pour into a baking-dish.
  10 We add the sugar to the beaten white of the egg, and place on top, and put in the oven to brown.
  11 When a light brown it is finished.
  12 When cool, place near the ice and serve cold.

### CORN-STARCH BLANC-MANGE.

1 We measure the milk, and put it to heat in a kettle of hot water.
2 We wet the corn-starch smooth with a little cold water.
3 We add it to the milk when it is just at boiling-point.
4 We stay by and stir until it tastes cooked.
5 We add the flavoring, sugar, and salt.
6 We rinse the mould or cup with cold water.
7 We pour in the pudding, and when cool set on the ice. Now it is finished.

## LESSON TENTH.

### DIAGRAM OF TABLES.

```
┌─────────────────────────────────────────────┐
│              TEACHER'S TABLE.                │
│                              Fancy Glass Dish,│
│      Salt,        Milk,      Platter,         │
│      Eggs,        Sugar.     Pudding-dish,    │
│      Flour.                  Extract,         │
│                              Nutmeg.          │
└─────────────────────────────────────────────┘
```

```
┌────────────────────────┐       ┌────────────────────────┐
│         |O             │       │         |O             │
│                        │       │                        │
│ O  Farina-kettle. or   │       │    Farina-kettle, or  O│
│ —  Saucepan and Pail,  │       │    Saucepan and Pail, —│
│    Table-spoon,        │       │    Small Platter,      │
│    Cup,                │       │    Two Forks and Bowl, │
│    Teaspoon,           │       │    Teaspoon,           │
│    Pint Measure.       │       │    Cup,                │
│                        │       │    Table-spoon.        │
│ O                      │       │                        │
│ —                      │       │                       O│
│                        │       │                       —│
│                        │       │                        │
│                        │       │                        │
│ O                      │       │                       O│
│ —                      │       │                       —│
│                        │       │                        │
│    Baking-dish,        │       │    Dripping-pan,       │
│    Grater,             │       │    Half doz. Custard-cups,│
│    Plate and Fork,     │       │    Pint Measure,       │
│ O  Bowl and Fork,      │       │    Nutmeg-grater,     O│
│ —  Table-spoon.        │       │    Bowl and Fork.     —│
│                        │       │                        │
│         O|             │       │         O|             │
└────────────────────────┘       └────────────────────────┘
```

```
        ┌─────────────────┐
        │     STOVE.      │
        │                 │
        │    Kettle.      │
        └─────────────────┘
```

# Music and Songs.

"WATCH THE OVEN WHEN YOU BAKE;
WHILE OTHERS SING, DON'T BURN THE CAKE."

## PINE FOR KINDLING.

SELECTED.

1. Pine for kind-ling is the best; Split some fine, leave coarse the rest. Put pa-per first to start the fire, Then pile the kind-ling on still higher. Lay them so crossed they'll let in air; To choke a fire is nev-er fair. Then

al - ways light it from be - low, That the flame may up - ward go.

  Catch the whole, and light the sticks,
  Then with care the coal you fix,
  Only take it with the shovel,
  As from a hod 'twill fall on double.
  For twenty minutes it is meet
  That the coal you oft repeat,
  But never pile it up so high,
  That the covers are too nigh;

  For it makes them warp and crack,
  When the stove you really pack.
  And best stoves are spoiled, 'tis said,
  If they get too hot and red.
  So at last the drafts you close,
  Your fire is made—but don't suppose,
  Your work is done, for still you must
  Brush up the hearth, wash up the dust.

## WASTE NOT.

SELECTED.

There's a du-ty all must learn, Du-ty to the ones who

earn: Du-ty, too, be-cause 'tis right, And from

CHORUS.

that there is no flight. Save the frag-ments, save them

all, Do not waste, how-ev-er small, Save the

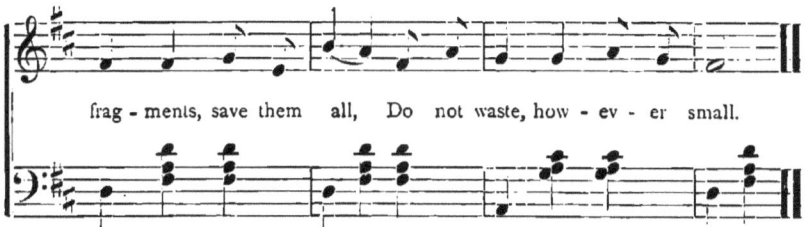

frag - ments, save them all, Do not waste, how - ev - er small.

We can give where there is need,
And the hungry help to feed:
Help with hand, and help with heart,
Do a sweet and christian part.

    CHO: Save the fragments, save them all,
           Do not waste, however small.

Many think to save is mean,
But how often it is seen,
Those who want are those who waste,
So such judgment is misplaced.

    CHO: Save the fragments, save them all,
           Do not waste, however small.

## COOKING GARDEN.

## BOILING POTATOES.

**SELECTED.**

1. If po-ta-toes you would boil, Cooking girls, cook-ing girls, And po-ta-toes would not spoil, cook-ing girls. You must o-pen wide your eyes, Get po-ta-toes of one size, Get po-

2 Then you pare them very thin, cooking girls, cooking girls,
   For the meal is next the skin, cooking girls.
   Cover them with water cold,
|: Pray remember what you're told, :|| cooking girls, cooking girls.

3 For a long time let them stay, cooking girls, cooking girls,
   Then the water turn away, cooking girls.
   Quick into the potato pot,
|: Pour the water boiling hot, :|| cooking girls, cooking girls.

4 Now let them boil to time, cooking girls, cooking girls,
   Watch for minutes twenty-nine, cooking girls.
   Sometimes it will take less,
|: Try with fork, and then you guess, :|| cooking girls, cooking girls.

5 Just as soon as they are soft, cooking girls, cooking girls,
   Then you pour the water off, cooking girls.
   Shake them well, and let them stay
|: Near the fire and steam away, :|| cooking girls, cooking girls.

6 Now that is "boiled potatoes" plain, cooking girls, cooking girls,
   When you mash them boil the same, cooking girls,
   Only crush them last, and beat,
|: In hot milk and butter sweet, :|| cooking girls, cooking girls.

## POTATO SONG.

SELECTED.

Tra la la la la la la, Tra la la la la.

The pretty bright green plants now bear,
 Tra la la, tra la la,
Most lovely flowers, we'd think, if rare,
 Tra la la la la.
And all the hills stand in a row,
And blooming make a charming show.
  Cho: Tra la la, etc.

When nature makes things beautiful,
 Tra la la, tra la la,
Should not we too be dutiful?
 Tra la la la la.
And if potatoes we prepare,
See that they show both taste and care.
  Cho: Tra la la, etc.

## BEATING EGGS.

SELECTED.

Beat-ing eggs, beat-ing eggs, Beat them from the ve-ry dregs;

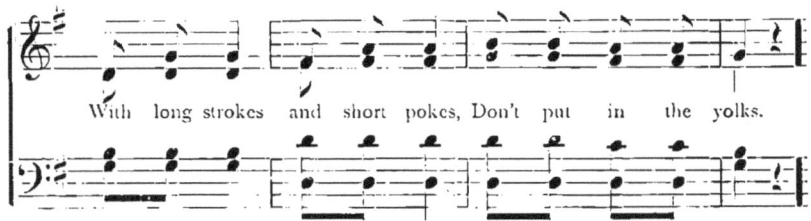

With long strokes and short pokes, Don't put in the yolks.

Beat them till they're ve-ry light, Beat a-way with all your might;

Shall we ev-er beat them so, Learn the song and know.

Here's a rule, here's a rule,
Taught us at our cooking school,
How to use, not abuse,
Eggs in different ways.
If a loaf of cake you make,
Then the egg with care you break,
For the white you beat light,
Till of mountain height.

Eggs you chop, eggs you chop,
With a spoon right through the top,
Yolk and white not too light
When you pudding make.
Still they must not stringy be,
Specks of white you must not see;
Beaten quite, but not too light,
To thicken milk is right.

## SALT SONG.

SELECTED.

3 Salt, salt must have a good savor,
  To give all our cooking its very best flavor;
  And girls who are careless of wrong and right doing,
  Are worthless as savorless salt.

## COOKING GARDEN.

# MEAT SONG.

**SELECTED.**

1. Meat is a food that we all of us use, Meat is a food that is, of-ten a-bused; Learn how to cook it, both taste-ful and nice, When to use sau-ces, and when to use spice.
2. One rule for all meats not made in-to a broth, Out-side you must seal, lest the jui-ces come forth, And on-ly great heat in the wa-ter or fat, In fire or ov-en is sure to do that.

## MARKETING SONG.

SELECTED.

## COOKING GARDEN.

## MUSIC AND SONGS.

Yes, 'tis Mar - ket Day! Yes, 'tis Mar - ket Day! Mar - ket Day!

Yes, 'tis Mar - ket Day! Yes, 'tis Mar - ket Day! Mar - ket Day!

2 Different kinds of meat we find,
    All on a market day;
And many fishes of every kind,
    Which shall we have, you say?
Nice roast beef rare, choose it with care,
    And beefsteak too, the whole year through,
Chicken, remember, October and November
    Cheap price you pay on a market day.

3 January, February, March, you will find
    All on a market day;
Mutton and pork, the best of the kind,
    All the butchers say.
Lamb chops, we're told, are cheapest sold,
    After September, this pray remember,
April and June, July and May,
    Veal is cheap on a market day.

MUSIC AND SONGS. 177

## HOME WELCOME.

Air—"*Araby's Daughter.*"   SELECTED.

1 { 'T is the du-ty of wo-men to make a house cheer-ful, A
    It is on-ly the des-o-late, for-lorn and tear-ful, That

rest to the fa-thers and moth-ers at home. } A
forc-es them ev-er for com-fort to roam.

bright bla-zing fire in the cold win-ter's chill, Or in

summer a sweet room where one can be still; And al-ways a welcome in

## COOKING GARDEN.

face and in mien. Di - rect from the heart it is ea - si - ly seen.

 2 How little we know of the worries and cares,
   Attending a business supporting us all;
  And she is at fault who for other calls spares
   The time or the talent to meet the home call.
  A bright pleasant story in the parlor, at table,
  May cause a good laugh, and thus you'll be able
  To make all the dear ones feel home is the best,
  That welcomes them always, and gives them true rest.

## BREAD MAKING SONG.

SELECTED.

{ Bring the board and bring the flour, Bring the roll-ing pin, }
{ Bring your cups and bring the measures, Bowl to make it in. }

Sift your flour with salt and su-gar In a pile so white,

Now we're rea-dy for the mould-ing, If the yeast is light.

2.
Scald the milk and heat the water,
    Cool till just luke-warm;
If too hot 't will kill the yeast-plant,
    That would do great harm.
If 'tis chilled, or too much heated,
    When you mould your bread,
It will leave the dough all heavy,
    For the yeast is dead.

3.
Make a deep hole in the middle,
    Like a little well,
There you pour your yeast and wa-
    How much you can tell.  [ter,

As you mix it from the edges,
    All the dry white flour,
Mixing softly, kneading after,
    For a half an hour.

4.
Now you place it in the bread bowl,
    A nice smooth dough ball,
Lard, a towel and a cover,
    And at night, that's all.
But when morning calls the sleeper,
    From her little bed,
She can make our breakfast biscuit,
    From the batch of bread.

## MAKING BISCUIT.

SELECTED.

1. Clear the ov-en, rake the fire, Pile the coal a lit-tle high-er, Let the heat grow firm and stea-dy, While we get the bis-cuit rea-dy. Bring-ing to the kitch-en ta-ble, Fast as lit-tle ones are a-ble,

2 Sift a quart of flour to fix it,
   With three spoons of powder mix it;
   Butter next, to do it rightly,
   Just egg sized, and rubbed in tightly.
   Add some salt, or you'll regret it,
   And a pint of milk to wet it;
   On the moulding-board now fold it.
   Gather gently, do not mould it.—Cho.

3 Roll and cut with nimble fingers,
   Shame upon the cook who lingers·
   Idle pains and trouble taking,
   When her biscuit should be baking.
   Now in buttered pan we've placed them,
   And let all who wish to taste them,
   Come in half an hour, we'll risk it,
   Well done, cook, and well done biscuit.—Cho.

## MUFFIN SONG.

SELECTED.

1. Sil - ly old hen, to tell it so plain, You've laid a new

egg, and you feel ve - ry vain. Lit - tle bright eyes, look

sharp in the hay, We want some fresh eggs for our

muf - fins to - day; Lit - tle bright eyes, look sharp in the

hay, We want some fresh eggs for our muf-fins to-day.

2 Plump little hands, you wash them all clean,
And roll up your sleeves till your elbows are seen;
Then in a large apron all cooks should be dressed,
And now you are ready to learn all the rest.

3 With flour sifted light, salt, milk and yeast,
You leave them all night—oh! what a great feast.
They must stand near the fire, all covered up tight,
With a cloth that is dainty and snowy and white.

4 Then when morning comes you beat light the eggs,
And mix with the batter, oh! mix from the dregs;
Then into the hot rings you pour them with care.
If browned to a turn, what with them can compare?

5 Now you and the hen have done what you could,
And made us a breakfast so light and so good.
But chick's lost her eggs, we've all had our fill:
Now don't you wish, chickie, that you had kept still?

## MOULDING SONG.

SELECTED.

1. Sing a song of six-pence, a bag full of rye, Four-and-twenty blackbirds baked in a pie; When the pie was opened the birds began to sing; Was not that a dainty dish to set before a king?

2 All the girls are learning how to mould the bread,
How to roll the cookies just as teacher said,
How to hold the cutter with the greatest care,
Making all their moulding fit for anywhere.

3 Clay we use for batter while we little know,
But as we get older, and the wiser grow,
Flour and meal you'll give us, for we've learned to-day
How to mix and mould them, kneading with the clay.

## VEGETABLE SONG.

SELECTED.

1. As rid-ing thro' the coun-try, one bright sum-mer day, I looked from the car-riage, And wished that in some way, I could car-ry back the pic-ture To the chil-dren of my care, Who were learn-ing so

186 *COOKING GARDEN.*

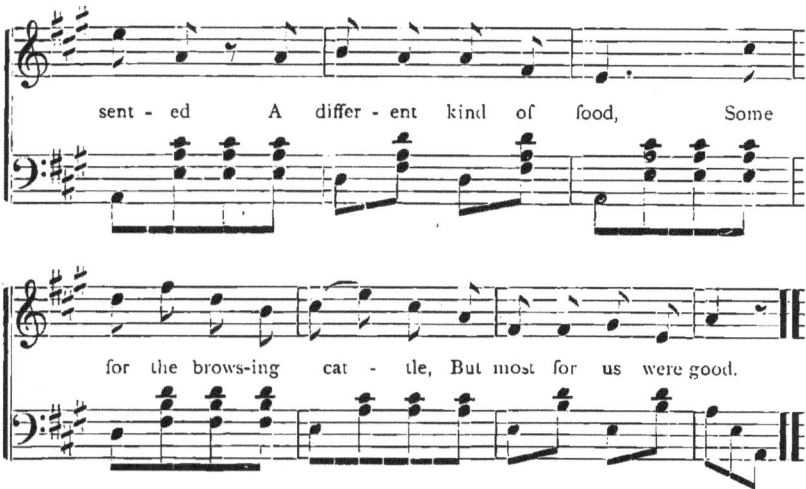

3  There were the useful seedlings,
    Like the wheat and graceful oats;
There were string beans and peas
    In their bright-green little coats;
And some grew very lowly—
    Indeed, beneath the ground ;
But with lovely blooming flowers
    Each little hill was crowned.

4  There were squashes in the garden,
    Tomatoes bright and red,
And light-green heads of lettuce,
    All gathered in a bed.
The fringy leaves of carrots
    A lovely contrast made,
And beneath the leaf, the cucumber
    Was resting in the shade.

5  Thus the vegetable creation
    Spoke loudly of the care
That in city or in country
    Is around us everywhere ;
But 'tis far more in the country
    We see our Father's hand :
In every glance His love is shown
    On every inch of land.

188 COOKING GARDEN.

## FISH SONG.

SELECTED.

1. Our les-son is fish, and in eve-ry dish, We would like to meet our teach-er's wish, But ma-ny men have ma-ny minds, There are ma-ny fish-es of ma-ny kinds; So we on-ly can learn to boil and bake, To broil and fry, and

make a fish cake, And trust this know-ledge will car-ry us through, When oth-er fish-es we have to do.

2  A napkin take and quickly make
   A little coat to fit the shape,
   And sew it very neatly in
   With thread and needle, not a pin.
   And thus it is a fish you boil;
   Without the coat 'twould break and spoil;
   And if you'd know when it is done,
   A knitting-needle through it run.

3  If fish you fry, it must be dry;
   The cooking-fat not rise too high.
   But heat must shut the juices in,
   And yet not scorch or break the skin.
   Of all the ways to cook a fish,
   To broil it is the healthiest dish.
   It soothes the nerves, the brain it feeds;
   So broil the fish, the doctor pleads.

190     *COOKING GARDEN.*

## A DAUGHTER AT HOME.

SELECTED.

1. Oh! what shall I do, for our cook has gone out; The hour of the dinner is coming about, Papa has sent word he'll bring friends home to dine, And he hopes that it all will be ready in time, And he hopes that it all will be ready in time; There's the

2  I will put on an apron as quick as I can;
   It would be such a shame to disappoint the dear man!
   And why need he know all the trials I've had?
   ‖: It only would trouble and make him feel sad. :‖
   ‖: I have learned how to place and serve every dish,
   Be it poultry or soup, or salad or fish. :‖
   By the time all is ready our maid will be here,
   And I'll meet my guests without any fear;
   For what is the use of a daughter at home,
   ‖: If for a good dinner a father must roam? :‖

## KATIE.

no one to wait on the bell at the door.

2 "This never will do," said our brave little Kate;
"The fire will go out and the dinner be late.
Both servants have left because mamma is ill,
So I must try her place and theirs too to fill;
For papa and brother will both look to me
To get them their dinner and mamma's hot tea.

3 "And I can do it, too, as my work will soon show;
We were taught all these things at the school where I go,
From the making of fire to the drawing of tea;
And knowing how makes it quite easy, you see.
I wonder I wasted so much time in crying,
When I'd only to rise and my school rules be trying."

4 So she closed up the drafts, shook the ashes away;
As she knew how to work, it was almost like play.
She put in the kindling to start up the fire,
And piled on the sticks just a little bit higher;
Then, opening the dampers, she lighted the match
And set fire to the papers, that easily catch.

5 And so she went on, this dear little maid;
Her lessons all kept her from being afraid.
When her heart failed, and she feared she was wrong,
She remembered the nice rules all written in song.
And when, on retiring, her papa she kissed,
He said that no comfort or care he had missed.

6 Now this is the moral from dear little Kate,
Who sets an example to every playmate:
We'll try to learn everything that girls can do.
What happens to Katie may not happen to you;
But in this world of changes we never can tell,
And you want to be ready to do your part well.

END OF FIRST COURSE.

## LAST WORDS.

I WOULD advise after this course additional lessons arranged on the same plan, teaching the following dishes, excellent receipts for which will be found in Miss Parloa's *Cook Book:*

Irish Stew, Fish Chowder, Picked up Codfish, Codfish Cakes, Pancakes, Mushes, Croquets, and the more ordinary Sauces.

After which I would recommend teaching the pupils to blend the dishes into simple meals from the lessons they have learned. This is necessary, as a great many persons have a nice understanding of each separate item in a bill of fare, who would be perplexed if obliged to harmonize them for a meal. In the latter part of Mrs. Whitney's *Just How*, the teacher would find great assistance in this matter. The following bills of fare for three breakfasts, three luncheons, and three dinners may be of service. The teacher's experience in the first course will guide her in the arrangement of quantities, diagrams, etc.

And I would feel keenly gratified if this book should not only help the volunteer teacher, but open a *profession* to educated women as well. With the excellent chemistries of food and large number of cook books published, and this simplified plan to guide, little cooking centers can be formed at a comparatively small expense. In a quiet way a dozen girls can be gathered around a cooking-stove and learn what will make their lives more valuable in any home, whatever capacity they may fill, whether as wife, mother, sister, or friend. This field is a large and important one, with great opportunities for development and extension. All entering it may be assured of the author's hearty co-operation and best wishes.

### BREAKFAST.

1 Warmed-over Meat, Fried Potatoes, Powder Biscuit, Coffee.

2 Fried Ham, Baked Potatoes, Scrambled Eggs, Water Toast.

3 Corn-beef Hash, Poached Eggs, Butter Balls, Coffee, Corn Bread.

#### LUNCHEON.

1 Mutton Chops, Stewed Potatoes, Raised Biscuit.
2 Beef Scallop, French Rolls, Cranberry Sauce, Tea.
3 Hash on Toast, Omelet, Fried Dough.

#### DINNER.

1 Tomato Soup, Roast Beef, Roast Potatoes, Cream Carrots, Rice Pudding.

2 Potato Soup, Mock Duck, Apple Sauce, Riced Potatoes, Boiled Custard.

3 Bean Soup, Broiled Steak, Mashed Potatoes (browned), Oyster-plant, Bread Pudding.

*₊* Illustrations on pages 5, 17, 31, 59, 155, and 195 are kindly loaned by the *St. Nicholas Magazine.*

THE END.

# THE
# WILSON INDUSTRIAL SCHOOL FOR GIRLS

[125 ST. MARK'S PLACE, NEW YORK]

Is NOT ENDOWED for its name, as its title suggests. It is unsectarian and sustained entirely by voluntary offerings. The names of the Board of Managers, to whom this book is dedicated, are a sufficient guarantee that contributions sent to their Treasurer will be fully appreciated and carefully expended.

## OFFICERS.

**First Directress.**
Mrs. JONATHAN STURGES, 40 East 36th Street.

**Second Directress.**
Mrs. LUTHER C. CLARK, 18 Gramercy Park.

**Treasurer.**
Mrs. AARON R. SMITH, New Brighton, Staten Island, N. Y.

**Secretary.**
Mrs. J. McLEAN HILDT, 39 West 20th Street.

**Managers.**

Mrs. E. BAYARD, 8 West 40th Street.
" ROBERT RUSSELL BOOTH, 7 West 16th St.
" T. M. LEWIS, 114 West 42d Street.
" J. S. BENNETT, 114 West 42d Street.
" H. H. G. SHARPLESS, 1st East 37th Street.
Miss DURKEE, 714 Fifth Avenue.
Mrs. G. E. KISSEL, 13 West 16th Street.
" GEO. C. CLARK, 7 West 37th Street.
" PAUL SPOFFORD, Hunt's Point.
" H. W. SIBLEY, 31 East 44th Street.

Mrs. A. F. DAMON, 187 Madison Avenue.
" R. W. HURLBUT, 43 West 29th Street.
Miss M. COLLINS, 41 West 11th Street.
" E. A. AUCHINCLOSS, 11 West 57th Street.
Mrs. H. O. HAVEMEYER, Stamford, Conn.
" J. L. SPOFFORD, Hunt's Point.
" GAMALIEL G. SMITH, 29 West 33d Street.
" CHARLES TAYLOR, 34 Gramercy Park.
" OLIVER B. JENNINGS, 49 Park Avenue.
" E. J. HAIGHT, Jr., 34 West 20th Street.

**Honorary Members.**

Mrs. JAMES P. WILSON, Newark, N. J.
" JOHN L. MASON, Downing Street, Brooklyn.

Miss C. NASH, 52 West 51st Street.
Mrs. J. VAN VECHTEN, 5 New Street.

**Advisory Committee.**

Rev. WM. T. SABINE.
T. S. HASTINGS, D.D.
C. D'W. BRIDGMAN, D.D.

WM. M. TAYLOR, D.D.
ROBERT RUSSELL BOOTH, D.D.
Rev. ARTHUR BROOKS.

**Building Committee.**

Mr. FREDERICK STURGES

Mr. THOMAS GARDNER.

www.ingramcontent.com/pod-product-compliance
Lightning Source LLC
Chambersburg PA
CBHW020932230426
43666CB00008B/1645